ANNE WILLAN'S
LOOK&COOK

Perfect Pies and Tarts

ANNE WILLAN'S
LOOK&COOK

Perfect Pies and Tarts

DORLING KINDERSLEY
LONDON • NEW YORK • STUTTGART

A DORLING KINDERSLEY BOOK

Created and Produced by
CARROLL & BROWN LIMITED
5 Lonsdale Road
London NW6 6RA

Editorial Director Jeni Wright
Editor Stella Vayne
Editorial Assistant Julia Alcock

Art Editor Lyndel Donaldson
Designers Alan Watt
Carmel O'Neill
Production Editor Wendy Rogers

First American Edition, 1994
10 9 8 7 6 5 4 3 2

Published in the United States by
Dorling Kindersley, Inc., 95 Madison Avenue
New York, New York 10016

Willan, Anne.
    Perfect Pies and Tarts / by Anne Willan. – 1st American ed.
    p.   cm. – (Look and cook)
    Includes index.
    ISBN 1-56458-506-9
    1. Pies. I. Title. II. Series: Willan, Anne. Look & cook.
TX773. W68 1994
641.8'652 – dc20   93–11616
                                                               CIP

Reproduced by Colourscan, Singapore
Printed and bound in Spain by Artes Gráficas Toledo, S.A.
D.L.TO:622-1994

CONTENTS

PIES AND TARTS

THE LOOK & COOK APPROACH

EQUIPMENT

INGREDIENTS

Welcome to **Perfect Pies and Tarts** and the *Look & Cook* series. These volumes are designed to be the most informative cookbooks you'll ever own. They are the closest I can come to sharing my techniques for cooking my own favorite recipes without actually being with you in the kitchen. Equipment and ingredients often determine whether or not you can cook a particular dish, so *Look & Cook* illustrates everything you need at the beginning of each recipe. You'll see at a glance how long a recipe takes to cook, how many servings it makes, what the finished dish looks like, and how much preparation can be done ahead. When you start to cook, you'll find the preparation and cooking are organized into easy-to-follow steps. Each stage has its own color coding and everything is shown in photographs with brief text accompanying each step. You will never be in doubt as to what it is you are doing, why you are doing it, and how it should look.

🍽 SERVES 4-6   🥄 WORK TIME 25-35 MINUTES   🍲 COOKING TIME 20-30 MINUTES

I've also included helpful hints and ideas under "Anne Says." These may list an alternative ingredient or piece of equipment, or explain the reason for using a certain method, or offer some advice on mastering a particular technique. Similarly, if there is a crucial stage in a recipe when things can go wrong, I've included some warnings called "Take Care."

Many of the photographs are annotated to pinpoint why certain pieces of equipment work best, or how food should look at the various stages of cooking. Because presentation is so important, there is a picture of the finished dish with serving suggestions at the end of each recipe.

Thanks to all this information, you can't go wrong. I'll be with you every step of the way. So please come with me into the kitchen to look, cook, and create some **Perfect Pies and Tarts**.

WHY PIES AND TARTS?

When is a pie a tart? A pie is often double-crusted or top-crusted. A tart is usually open. Much depends on national origin – pies, made with shortcrust and pie pastry, are British and American, while tarts, made with pâte sucrée and puff pastry, tend to be French. Whatever the origin, there's a perfect pie or tart for every occasion.

RECIPE CHOICE

The wide choice of pastries and fillings for pies and tarts leads to an almost infinite variety of combinations. In this book are many of my favorites, chosen to allow you to master as many new techniques as possible. Familiar rounds of plain pie dough are just a beginning – you will find pies, tarts, and tartlets in an exciting range of shapes and sizes. Some are international, such as Fig and Mulled Wine Tart from Italy and Plum Tart from Bavaria. Levels of difficulty range from simple Double-Crust Apple Pie or Classic Pecan Pie to more advanced puff pastry tartlets.

PIES AND TARTS

English Blackberry and Apple Pie: blackberries and apples have a natural affinity, and are combined in a traditional English deep-dish pie. *Victorian Plum Pie:* a generous filling of purple plums and crunchy toasted walnuts bakes beneath a decorative lid of shortcrust pastry. *Cherry Tartlets:* luscious cherries on a cream cheese filling in individual cases of sweet pastry. *Baked Cherry Tartlets:* sour cream and eggs are added to the cream cheese filling so that it puffs lightly around the succulent cherries during baking. *Lemon Meringue Pie:* a cloud of meringue crowns the tangy lemon curd filling of this enduringly popular pie. *Cranberry Meringue Pie:* bright red, sharp-tasting cranberries provide flavor and color contrast to a topping of white Italian meringue. *Spirited Eggnog Pie:* the ingredients of eggnog, vanilla, nutmeg, and rum, are added to a custard that is set in a crust made from ground or crushed Amaretti cookies. *Irish Coffee Tartlets:* the hot after-dinner drink is transformed into a cold filling for tartlets topped with rosettes of Chantilly cream. *Double-Crust Rhubarb and Strawberry Pie:* the season for tender rhubarb and garden strawberries coincides, leading to this double-crusted pie in which the fruit juices are lightly

thickened with flour. *Double-Crust Apple Pie:* this American classic is best served hot, perhaps with a scoop of ice cream, *à la mode,* or with a slice of Cheddar cheese. *Lemon Tart:* sweet orange softens the sharpness of lemon, with candied lemon slices as a fitting decoration. *Lime and Cardamom Tart:* rosettes of Chantilly cream mellow the tang of lime, while cardamom imparts exotic subtlety. *Pear Pie with Walnut Pastry:* wedges of pear are sandwiched between sweet walnut pastry in this specialty of central France. *Peach Pie with Walnut Pastry:* a pie for summer, when peaches are at their juicy best. *Chocolate Pye with a Crunchy Crust:* in this tart dating back to eighteenth century England, a velvety chocolate filling contrasts with a crisp almond crust. *Chocolate and Chestnut Pye with a Crunchy Crust:* nuggets of chestnut add texture to a rich chocolate cream filling, set in an almond crust. *Chocolate Mint Pye with a Crunchy Crust:* fresh mint gives a refreshing highlight to the richness of the chocolate filling. *Strawberry Mousse Pie:* deep brown chocolate crust surrounds an airy pink filling, a cross between strawberry mousse and soufflé, highlighted by a decoration of strawberry fans. *Coconut Mousse Pie:* coconut milk and toasted shredded coconut are the ideal complement for a chocolate crust. *Amelia Simmons' Molasses Pumpkin Pie:* flavored with blackstrap molasses, ground ginger, nutmeg, and mace, this recipe is inspired by the author of the first American cookbook, written in 1796. *Pumpkin Crunch Pie:* for this autumn favorite, the pumpkin is spiced with ground nutmeg, cinnamon, and allspice, then covered with a pecan topping.

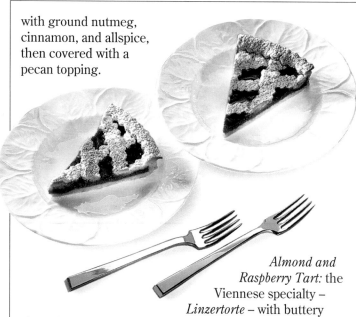

Almond and Raspberry Tart: the Viennese specialty – *Linzertorte* – with buttery almond pastry, a dense filling of fresh raspberries, and a pretty pastry lattice. *Hazelnut and Apricot Tart:* sweet hazelnut pastry holds a chunky purée of dried apricots in a dessert tart that is perfect with coffee. *Braided Three-Nut Pie:* decorative pastry braids border a rich sweet filling of walnuts, hazelnuts, and almonds, bound with eggs and brown sugar. *Classic Pecan Pie:* the all-American dessert. *Caramelized Upside-Down Mango Tartlets:* in this contemporary version of the famous upside-down apple tart – *Tarte Tatin* – mango slices and caramel are combined under a sweet pastry lid, which becomes the base when the tartlets are turned out after baking. *Caramelized Upside-Down Peach Tart:* peaches are steeped in caramel in this spectacular upside-down tart. *Triple-Decker Dried Peach Tart:* when layers of pâte brisée and dried peaches are cut, an attractive striped slice is revealed. *Triple-Decker Prune Tart:* in this regional recipe from Gascony, prunes soaked in Armagnac are layered with pâte brisée. *Fresh Mincemeat Tart:* fresh apple and grapes are added to dried fruit for a light, up-to-date version of an old-fashioned favorite. *Festive Mincemeat Tart:* packed with dried fruit, this traditional holiday tart deserves to be eaten throughout the year. *Flaky Pear Tartlets:* a sensational combination of golden puff pastry, warm caramelized pears, and Chantilly cream. *Flaky Apple Tartlets:* caramelized apples, buttery puff pastry, and whipped Chantilly cream guarantee approval. *Fig and Mulled Wine Tart:* cornmeal adds texture and taste to a pastry that is topped with lightened pastry cream and fresh figs poached in spiced red wine. *Fig and Mulled Wine Tartlets:* freeform cornmeal pastry rounds are topped with sliced fresh figs. *Mud Pie:* this decadent dessert of coffee ice cream, rippled with almond-studded fudge sauce, is set in a chocolate crumb crust, topped with whipped cream and almonds, and served with hot fudge sauce. *Gingersnap Ice Cream Pie:* smooth ice cream, spiced with crystallized ginger and swirled with fudge sauce, is piled into a crisp gingersnap crust. *Bavarian Plum Tart:* a quick version of buttery brioche makes an ideal container for juicy plums, baked in a light custard. *Bavarian Blueberry Tart:* plump, juicy blueberries, together with a light custard, complement the brioche crust. *Apple Jalousie:* fresh ginger root spices the apple filling of this French pastry with a slashed top that resembles the louvers of a shutter or *jalousie*. *Banana Shuttles:* bananas moistened with rum, then dipped in sugar, make a happy union with butter-rich puff pastry. *Hazelnut, Chocolate, and Orange Tart:* Italian sweet pastry dough is filled with a hazelnut, chocolate, and candied orange mixture, then finished with a chocolate glaze to guarantee that your meal ends on a special note. *Chocolate and Walnut Truffle Tart:* cocoa powder dusts the smooth chocolate glaze of this nutty tart, reminiscent of chocolate truffles. *Pistachio and Ricotta Phyllo Pie:* a box of crisp, wafer-thin phyllo pastry encloses layers of pistachio nuts and lemon-flavored ricotta cheese studded with raisins. *Poppy Seed Phyllo Pie:* ingredients from eastern Europe come together in a deliciously satisfying pie. *Fresh Fruit Tartlets:* a colorful combination of fresh fruit is displayed to perfection in flaky, crisp puff pastry shells lined with pastry cream. *Mixed Berry Tart:* an easy-to-serve band of puff pastry topped with Grand Marnier-flavored pastry cream and a trio of fresh berries.

EQUIPMENT

The basis of all pies and tarts is pastry, and the most vital "tool" for making it is your hands. If your hands or the kitchen are warm, soak your hands briefly in cold water or chill the work surface by leaving a tray of ice cubes on top for a few minutes before you start. A plastic or metal pastry scraper combines the ingredients for pâte sucrée and pâte brisée with a minimum of handling, and the wires of a pastry blender cut butter and shortening into the flour for shortcrust pastry without warming the fat. A food processor is a useful alternative to your hands in pastry-making, and its use is also described and illustrated.

For shaping pastry you will need a rolling pin, and a knife to trim edges without crushing the layered structure of a delicate dough, such as puff pastry. A plain or fluted pastry wheel can do the job as well. With a pastry brush, it is easy to add an even layer of glaze to your dough, and to coat pans and plates with melted butter to prevent sticking.

To give pies and tarts the desired shape and ensure that they bake evenly and thoroughly, it is essential to use pans of the correct shape and size. These vary from French-style metal tart pans, with removable bases that make unmolding easy, to traditional American heatproof glass pie plates with sloping sides. Quiche dishes are often deeper, with fluted sides, and are made of ceramic material. Note that the diameter of pans is normally measured at the widest point of the rim.

Specialty molds include the oval English deep pie dish for Blackberry and Apple Pie and Victorian Plum Pie, fluted individual brioche molds for Cherry Tartlets and Baked Cherry Tartlets, and ceramic ovenproof individual dishes for Caramelized Upside-Down Mango Tartlets.

A heated heavy baking sheet under a pastry shell ensures that the pastry will be crisp. Dried beans or rice weight a pastry shell when it is "blind" baked without filling, so that it will not become soggy when filled. A wire rack allows air to circulate beneath a baked pie as it cools, thereby speeding cooling time, and helping a crisp base to stay crisp.

The range of equipment for making fillings encompasses everyday kitchen items, such as bowls, wooden spoons, a citrus juicer, grater, chef's knife, small knife, vegetable peeler, and chopping board. You'll also need a whisk for whipping heavy cream and for making fillings, such as pastry cream. When making Italian meringue, you can use a candy thermometer to check the temperature of sugar syrup but a hand test is described in the relevant recipe. For making decorations with meringue and whipped cream, a pastry bag fitted with a star tube is almost indispensable.

As always, machines will speed and ease your work. A food processor or blender is useful for grinding nuts and puréeing fillings, an electric mixer for making light-as-air meringue. An ice cream maker is needed for Mud Pie, and a spice or coffee grinder for Poppy Seed Phyllo Pie.

INGREDIENTS

The staple ingredients of pies and tarts are flour and butter. Because the final taste of the pastry is so important, I prefer to use unsalted butter for its superior flavor. In American pie pastry, the fat used is vegetable shortening, which contributes less taste than butter but has an agreeably light texture. In English shortcrust pastry, the two fats are combined for the best of both worlds.

The flour used for all these recipes is unbleached all-purpose flour. The gluten (which gives elasticity to dough) and moisture content of the flour may vary from batch to batch, so the amount of water or other liquid that you must add when mixing dough is always approximate. Egg yolks are added to the French pastries, pâte brisée and pâte sucrée, helping to bind the dough and give richness of flavor and color.

In most sweet pastries, granulated sugar is appropriate because its fine grains dissolve readily, leaving the pastry smooth. Note that a high proportion of sugar makes pastry dough much more difficult to handle, with the danger of scorching when the sugar starts to caramelize in the oven. Cocoa powder or finely ground nuts are other ingredients added to enrich doughs. You'll find cocoa powder in Strawberry Mousse Pie, walnuts in Pear Pie with Walnut Pastry, and an almond dough in Chocolate Pye with a Crunchy Crust. The freshness of nuts is important, particularly if you buy them already ground, because they can develop a rancid flavor when stale.

Fillings for pies and tarts must be full of character to contrast with the pastry background. Acid fruit, such as lemons, rhubarb, and strawberries, are favorites. Less vivid fruit, like peaches, mangoes, and figs, often have caramel or spices, a dash of alcohol, and other pick-me-ups added. The texture of a filling is equally important, and here nuts come into their own, adding both flavor and a crunchy texture. Alternatively, a filling may be richly smooth with chocolate, cream, or cream cheese, or fluffy with whipped eggs. The ideas in this book are just a beginning.

ENGLISH BLACKBERRY AND APPLE PIE

  SERVES 4–6   WORK TIME 35–40 MINUTES*   BAKING TIME 50–60 MINUTES

EQUIPMENT

1-quart oval pie dish †

citrus juicer

large metal spoon

pastry brush

strainer

bowls

pastry blender ‡

pie funnel

melon baller

chef's knife

1-inch round cookie cutter

vegetable peeler

small knife

rolling pin

metal skewer

chopping board

† shallow baking dish can also be used

‡ 2 round-bladed table knives can also be used

ANNE SAYS
"If you use a shallow dish, cut petal-shaped steam vents in the center of the dough to let steam escape."

Blackberries and apples combine well, ripening together as an early autumn treat. Use a tart apple, such as Granny Smith or Jonathan, for this pie, which is topped with shortcrust pastry – the English equivalent of pie pastry. The pie is best served warm, with chilled heavy cream.

GETTING AHEAD

The shortcrust pastry dough can be made up to 2 days ahead and kept, tightly wrapped, in the refrigerator. The pie is best eaten the day it is baked.

*plus 45 minutes chilling time

SHOPPING LIST

1½ pints	blackberries
1¾ lb	tart apples
1	lemon
¾ cup	sugar, more to taste
	For the shortcrust pastry dough
1½ cups	flour
1½ tbsp	sugar (optional)
¼ tsp	salt
¼ cup	vegetable shortening
¼ cup	unsalted butter
3–4 tbsp	cold water, more if needed

INGREDIENTS

blackberries

tart apples

unsalted butter

vegetable shortening

flour

sugar

lemon

ANNE SAYS
"Frozen blackberries can also be used, provided they are drained of juice after they have been defrosted."

ORDER OF WORK

1 **MAKE THE PASTRY DOUGH; PREPARE THE PIE FILLING**

2 **ASSEMBLE THE PIE**

3 **DECORATE AND BAKE THE PIE**

1 MAKE THE PASTRY DOUGH; PREPARE THE PIE FILLING

1 Make the shortcrust pastry dough (see box, page 12). While it is chilling, pick over the blackberries; wash them only if dirty. Squeeze the lemon, and set the juice aside.

2 Peel the apples with the vegetable peeler. Cut out the stem and flower ends from each apple.

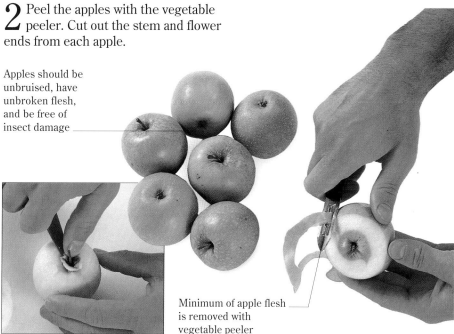

Apples should be unbruised, have unbroken flesh, and be free of insect damage

Minimum of apple flesh is removed with vegetable peeler

3 Halve 1 apple, and scoop out the core from each half with the melon baller. Repeat for the remaining apples.

4 Set 1 apple half, cut-side down, on the chopping board. Cut it lengthwise in half, then slice it crosswise into 6 chunks. Repeat for the remaining apple halves.

Toss apples with lemon juice and sugar first, to avoid crushing blackberries

More sugar may be needed if fruit is very tart

5 Put the apples in a bowl. Add the lemon juice and all but 2 tbsp of the sugar; toss to combine. Reserve the 2 tbsp sugar for the topping.

6 Add the blackberries to the apple chunks, and toss again lightly. Taste the fruit mixture, adding more sugar if necessary.

HOW TO MAKE SHORTCRUST PASTRY DOUGH

Shortcrust pastry dough is a sturdy flaky pastry that lends itself to a variety of pies and tarts. Following English tradition, butter is used in the dough for flavor. For a light dough, chill the shortening and butter, and handle the dough as little as possible.

Working fat with pastry blender instead of your fingers keeps it cool

Work mixture to form bean-sized pieces

1 Sift the flour, sugar, if using, and salt into a medium bowl.

2 Cut the chilled shortening and butter into pieces, and add to the flour mixture; then cut into the mixture with a pastry blender or with 2 round-bladed table knives.

3 Rub in the fat with your fingertips until the mixture forms coarse crumbs, lifting and crumbling to help aerate it.

4 Sprinkle the water over the mixture, 1 tbsp at a time, and mix lightly with a fork.

! TAKE CARE !
Do not use too much water, or the dough will be sticky and the pastry tough.

5 Continue mixing with the fork until the crumbs are moist enough to start sticking together.

ANNE SAYS
"The fork keeps the mixture cool, and the fat from melting into the flour."

6 Press the dough lightly into a ball, wrap it tightly, and chill until firm, about 30 minutes.

Dough comes together easily to form soft, but not sticky, ball

Handle dough lightly at this stage

2 ASSEMBLE THE PIE

1 Lightly flour the work surface. Roll out the chilled dough, and trim to an oval 3 inches larger than the top of the pie dish. Reserve the trimmings.

2 Invert the pie dish on the dough. Cut a ¾-inch strip from the edge, leaving an oval 1½ inches larger than the dish.

Use tip of small sharp knife

Sugar has drawn out juice from fruit

3 Set the pie dish, right-side up, on the work surface. Place the pie funnel in the center of the pie dish and spoon the fruit around it.

ANNE SAYS
"The fruit filling should be mounded in the dish; it will reduce during baking."

Pie funnel helps support crust and allows steam to escape through hole in center

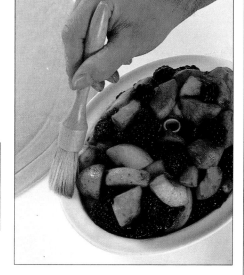

4 With the pastry brush, lightly moisten the edge of the pie dish with cold water.

5 Lift the strip from around the oval of dough, and transfer it to the edge of the pie dish, pressing it down firmly.

Moistening with water helps seal dough strip to lid of dough

6 Trim the strip, if necessary, so that it is even with the edge of the pie dish, reserving any trimmings. Brush the strip with cold water.

7 Roll up the oval of dough around the rolling pin and unroll it over the pie filling. Press the edge down onto the dough strip to seal it. With the tip of the small knife, cut a small hole in the dough over the pie funnel, to allow steam to escape.

Rolling pin is lightly floured, so dough does not stick

Drape dough gently over fruit so it does not stretch

8 Trim the dough edge, lifting the dish on your hand. Reserve the trimmings to make leaves, flowers, and berries to decorate the pie.

3 DECORATE AND BAKE THE PIE

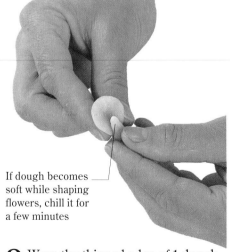

If dough becomes soft while shaping flowers, chill it for a few minutes

1 Roll out the dough trimmings. Cut strips of dough about 1-inch wide and cut them into leaf shapes. Mark veins on 1 leaf with the back of the small knife, brush the base with cold water, and press it onto the pie center, curving it with your fingers. Repeat, placing leaves around the pie center, and at each end.

2 To make 2 pastry flowers, stamp out 10 small rounds from the dough with the cookie cutter. Squeeze one edge of each round to thin it out a little. Set the rounds aside. With your fingertips, roll 2 small pieces of dough into 1-inch lengths to make the flower centers around which to wrap the pastry dough petals.

3 Wrap the thinned edge of 1 dough round around 1 flower center, and pinch gently to make it stick to the center. Slightly overlap the first round with a second round, and pinch to make it stick. Repeat with 3 more dough rounds so that there are 5 flower petals wrapped around the flower center. Bend the petals outward slightly to shape.

4 Trim the excess dough from the base of the flower. Brush the base with cold water, and press it onto the leaves at one edge of the pie. Make a second flower, and press it onto the leaves at the opposite edge.

5 For the berries, roll tiny balls of dough with your fingertips, brush with a little cold water, and press onto the pie in clusters. Chill the pie until firm, about 15 minutes. Meanwhile, heat the oven to 375°F.

6 Bake the pie in the heated oven until the pastry is lightly browned and crisp, and the apples are tender when pierced with the metal skewer, 50–60 minutes. Remove the pie from the oven, and immediately sprinkle with the reserved sugar.

¶⚬¶ TO SERVE
Serve the pie hot or warm, with heavy cream as an accompaniment, if you like.

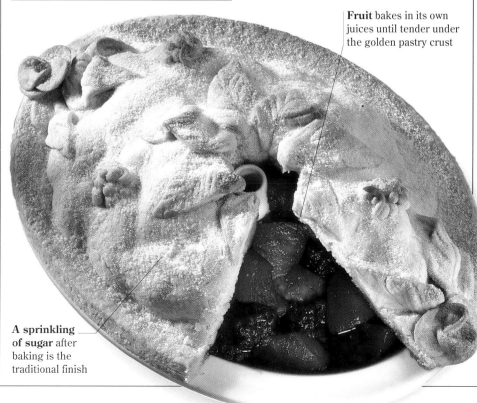

Fruit bakes in its own juices until tender under the golden pastry crust

A sprinkling of sugar after baking is the traditional finish

V A R I A T I O N

VICTORIAN PLUM PIE

This pie is named for the Victoria, a plum first planted in Britain in the nineteenth century.

1 Omit the apples and blackberries. Make the shortcrust pastry dough as directed. Heat the oven to 350°F. Spread 1 cup walnut pieces in an even layer on a baking sheet and toast in the heated oven until lightly browned, stirring occasionally, so that they color evenly, 8–10 minutes. Increase the oven temperature to 375°F.
2 Halve and pit 2½ lb purple plums: with a small, sharp knife, cut each plum in half, using the indentation on one side as a guide. Twist with both hands to loosen the plum halves; then pull them apart. If the flesh clings, loosen it from the plum pit with a knife. Scoop out the pit with the point of the knife, and discard it. Repeat for the remaining plums.
3 In a medium bowl, combine the plums, toasted walnuts, and ½ cup sugar; taste, and add more sugar if you like. Assemble the pie as directed.
4 Roll out the dough trimmings. Cut out stem and leaf shapes. Round the stems by rolling them between your fingertips, brush with cold water, and gently press onto the pie. Use the back of the small knife to mark the leaves with long veins. Brush the base of each leaf with water, then gently curve and press onto the pastry stems. Add a few dough berries, if you like. Bake the pie as directed. While the pie is still hot, sprinkle with 2 tbsp sugar.

CHERRY TARTLETS

🍽 SERVES 8   🥣 WORK TIME 40–45 MINUTES*   🍲 BAKING TIME 20–25 MINUTES

EQUIPMENT

pastry scraper

eight 3-inch diameter brioche molds †

pastry brush

vegetable peeler

strainer

bowls

4-inch round cookie cutter

grater

pastry bag and large star tube

electric mixer ‡

wire rack

small saucepan

baking sheet

parchment paper

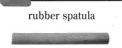
rubber spatula

rolling pin

† muffin pans can also be used
‡ wooden spoon can also be used

In this Bavarian recipe, cherries top a delicious cream cheese filling, set in pâte sucrée shells. Berries, such as raspberries, strawberries, or blueberries can be substituted for the cherries.

GETTING AHEAD

The shells and filling can be prepared 1 day ahead. Keep shells in an airtight container and filling in the refrigerator. Assemble not more than 1–2 hours before serving.

*plus 1 hour chilling time

SHOPPING LIST

³⁄₄ lb	cherries
1	lemon
¹⁄₂ lb	cream cheese
3 tbsp	sugar
¹⁄₂ tsp	vanilla extract
¹⁄₂ cup	heavy cream
8	small sprigs of fresh mint for decoration
	For the pâte sucrée dough
1¹⁄₂ cups	flour, more if needed
6 tbsp	unsalted butter, more for brioche molds
¹⁄₃ cup	sugar
¹⁄₂ tsp	vanilla extract
¹⁄₄ tsp	salt
3	egg yolks
	For the glaze
¹⁄₃ cup	red currant jelly
1 tbsp	kirsch

INGREDIENTS

cherries

lemon

flour

cream cheese

egg yolks

unsalted butter

vanilla extract

sugar

heavy cream

red currant jelly †

kirsch ‡

mint sprigs

† cherry jelly can also be used
‡ water can also be used

ORDER OF WORK

1. **MAKE THE PÂTE SUCRÉE DOUGH; LINE AND BLIND BAKE THE TARTLET SHELLS**

2. **PREPARE THE CHERRIES AND MAKE THE FILLING**

3. **ASSEMBLE THE TARTLETS**

1 MAKE THE PATE SUCREE DOUGH; LINE AND BLIND BAKE THE TARTLET SHELLS

1 Make and chill the pâte sucrée dough (see box, page 18). Melt the butter, then brush 4 of the brioche molds with melted butter.

2 Lightly flour the work surface. Roll out two-thirds of the chilled pâte sucrée dough so it is $1/8$-inch thick. Return the remaining dough to the refrigerator. Cut out 4 rounds with the cookie cutter: they should be large enough to line the molds completely.

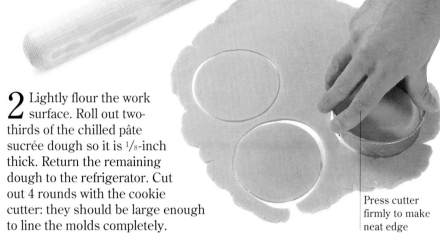

Press cutter firmly to make neat edge

3 With your thumb, press 1 round well into the bottom and up the side of a mold to form a neat pastry shell. Repeat for the remaining rounds. Add the dough trimmings to the remaining one-third dough.

4 Prick the bottom of each pastry shell with a fork to prevent air bubbles from forming during baking. Chill the shells until firm, about 15 minutes. Heat the oven to 400°F. Put the baking sheet in the oven to heat.

5 Carefully line each of the pastry shells with a second mold, so that they keep their shape during baking.

6 Bake on the baking sheet in the heated oven until set and the rims start to brown, 6–8 minutes. Remove the lining molds, and reduce the oven temperature to 375°F. Continue baking the shells until the dough is thoroughly cooked and golden brown, 3–5 minutes longer.

Shell should be firm and just starting to brown

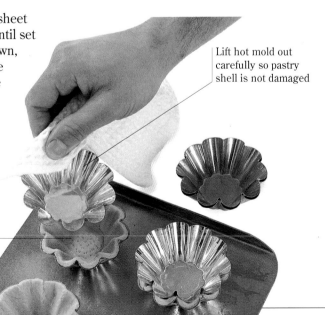

Lift hot mold out carefully so pastry shell is not damaged

7 Unmold and transfer each pastry shell to the wire rack to cool. Let the molds cool. Roll out the remaining dough, line the molds, chill, and bake 4 more pastry shells in the same way.

HOW TO MAKE PATE SUCREE DOUGH

The favorite French sweet pastry is pâte sucrée. The high proportion of sugar and egg yolks gives the dough a crumbly character, much like a cookie. The dough can also be made in a food processor (see box, page 76).

1 Sift the flour onto the work surface, and make a well in the center. Pound the butter with the rolling pin to soften it.

2 Put the sugar, softened butter, vanilla extract, salt, and egg yolks into the well.

Well in flour is large enough for ingredients to be mixed easily

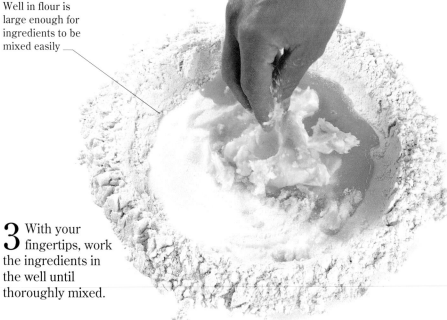

3 With your fingertips, work the ingredients in the well until thoroughly mixed.

4 Draw in the flour with the pastry scraper, then work the flour into the other ingredients with your fingers until coarse crumbs form.

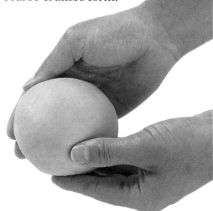

5 With your fingers, press the crumbs firmly together to form a ball of dough. If the dough is sticky, work in a little more flour. Lightly flour the work surface.

6 Blend the dough by pushing it away from you with the heel of your hand, then gathering it up, until it is very smooth and peels away from the work surface, 1–2 minutes.

7 Shape the dough into a ball, wrap it tightly, and chill until firm, about 30 minutes.

2 PREPARE THE CHERRIES AND MAKE THE FILLING

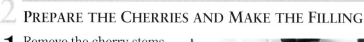

1 Remove the cherry stems, and scoop out the pits with the tip of the vegetable peeler. Set the cherries aside while making the filling.

Choose firm unblemished cherries

Point of vegetable peeler does least damage to cherry

Discard stems as well as pits

Cream cheese softens quickly with electric mixer

2 Grate the zest from the lemon onto parchment paper, taking care not to grate into the bitter white pith.

ANNE SAYS
"Use a brush to remove zest remaining on the grater."

3 With the electric mixer, beat the cream cheese until soft. Add the vanilla extract, sugar, and lemon zest to the cream cheese, and beat until light and fluffy, 2–3 minutes.

4 Pour the heavy cream into a chilled bowl, and whip with the electric mixer until soft peaks form.

5 Add the whipped heavy cream to the cream cheese mixture, and fold together with the rubber spatula until well mixed. Cover and chill while making the glaze and glazing the tartlet shells.

3 ASSEMBLE THE TARTLETS

1 Make the red currant jelly glaze (see box, right). Brush the inside of each pastry shell with glaze.

Glaze must be warm so it spreads evenly

ANNE SAYS
"The jelly glaze protects the tartlet shells from the moist cheese filling so they stay crisp longer."

2 Drop the star tube into the pastry bag and twist, tucking the bag into the tube. Fold the top of the bag over your hand, and add the chilled filling, using the rubber spatula.

Apply even pressure when piping

Glazed tartlet shells retain crispness

3 Twist the top of the bag until there is no air left in it. Hold the twisted top of the bag between your thumb and forefinger, and squeeze the bag to pipe the filling into the tartlet shells, filling them three-quarters full, with a rosette in the center.

HOW TO MAKE A FRUIT JELLY OR JAM GLAZE

A jelly or jam glaze is brushed on fruit to make it glisten and keep it moist; it also adds flavor. Use red currant jelly as a glaze for red fruit; apricot jam for green and yellow fruit. A glaze can also be brushed in a pastry shell to keep the filling from making pastry soggy.

Put the jelly or jam in a small saucepan with water or other liquid. Heat gently, stirring occasionally, until the glaze is melted. Use the glaze while warm and easy to spread with a brush.

ANNE SAYS
"If using apricot jam, work the glaze through a strainer and melt again."

4 Arrange the cherries in a circle on top of the filling in each of the tartlet shells, leaving the rosette in the center uncovered.

5 Brush the cherries with the remaining glaze, making sure it does not drip onto the filling.

🍴 **TO SERVE**

Decorate each tartlet with a small mint sprig, and transfer to a serving platter. Serve chilled, or at room temperature.

V A R I A T I O N

BAKED CHERRY TARTLETS

In this version of Cherry Tartlets, sour cream and egg enrich a cherry-studded filling baked in the pastry shells.

1 Omit the heavy cream from the filling. Make and chill the pâte sucrée dough, cut dough rounds, and line 4 brioche molds as directed. Chill, then line each pastry shell with a second mold as directed.

2 Blind bake the pastry shells as directed, 6–8 minutes. Unmold and cool as directed, and repeat for the remaining 4 pastry shells. Reduce the oven temperature to 350°F.

3 Stem and pit ³/₄ lb cherries. Make the filling: beat ¹/₄ lb cream cheese until soft; beat in ¹/₃ cup sour cream, 1 egg, and 2 tbsp sugar with the lemon zest and vanilla extract.

4 Replace the pastry shells in the molds. Spoon the filling into the shells, top with the cherries, and bake the tartlets in the heated oven until the filling is firm, 25–30 minutes. Let the tartlets cool to room temperature on the wire rack, then unmold them.

5 Serve the tartlets chilled, or at room temperature, and dust the top of each tartlet with confectioners' sugar just before serving.

Sweet pastry bakes to a cookie-like crispness

Cream cheese filling offsets the juicy sweetness of cherries

LEMON MERINGUE PIE

 SERVES 6–8 **WORK TIME 45–50 MINUTES*** **BAKING TIME 10–12 MINUTES***

EQUIPMENT

bowls, 1 metal

pastry bag and large star tube

wire rack

9-inch pie plate

baking sheet

electric mixer

kitchen scissors

wooden spoon

metal spatula

whisk

citrus juicer

parchment paper

pastry brush

chef's knife

rolling pin

aluminum foil

grater

saucepans, 1 heavy-based

dried beans

small strainer

medium strainer

It is not surprising that lemon meringue pie has achieved international renown. Tart lemon curd crowned with sweet meringue peaks is a time-honored combination few can resist.

GETTING AHEAD

The pastry shell can be baked and the lemon curd made 1 day ahead. Keep the pastry shell in an airtight container, and the curd covered in the refrigerator. Assemble the pie, and broil the meringue up to 2 hours before serving.

plus 45 minutes chilling
**plus 20–25 minutes blind baking*

SHOPPING LIST

5	lemons
3	egg yolks
2	eggs
1/2 cup	unsalted butter, more for pie plate
3/4 cup	sugar
	For the pie pastry dough
1 1/2 cups	flour
1 1/2 tbsp	sugar (optional)
1/2 tsp	salt
1/2 cup	vegetable shortening
3–4 tbsp	cold water, more if needed
	For the Italian meringue
1/2 cup	sugar
1/3 cup	water
3	egg whites

INGREDIENTS

egg yolks

sugar

flour

egg whites

lemons

eggs

unsalted butter

vegetable shortening

ORDER OF WORK

1. **MAKE THE PIE PASTRY DOUGH; SHAPE AND BLIND BAKE THE PASTRY SHELL**

2. **MAKE THE LEMON CURD**

3. **MAKE THE ITALIAN MERINGUE AND FINISH THE PIE**

MAKE THE PIE PASTRY DOUGH; SHAPE AND BLIND BAKE THE PASTRY SHELL

Use pie plate to measure dough

1 Make and chill the dough (see box, page 69), adding sugar, if using, with the flour. Brush the pie plate with melted butter. On a floured surface, roll dough into a round 2 inches larger than the top of the pie plate.

2 Using the rolling pin, drape the dough over the plate.

3 Gently lift the edge of the dough with your fingertips, and press it well into the bottom and up the side of the pie plate. Press to seal any cracks in the dough.

4 Using the kitchen scissors or a table knife, trim the dough so that it extends ³/₈-inch out from the edge of the plate.

Pinch dough gently with your thumbs to make fluted edge

5 Fold under the excess dough to make a thicker edge. Flute the edge of the pastry shell: press your thumbs together diagonally into the edge to make a ridge. Continue around the edge in this way until the fluting is completed.

6 Prick the bottom of the pastry shell with a fork to prevent air bubbles from forming during cooking. Chill until firm, about 15 minutes. Blind bake the shell (see box, page 24). Leave the oven temperature at 375°F, and leave the baking sheet in the oven.

HOW TO BLIND BAKE A PASTRY SHELL

Shells are often partially baked, or completely baked, before a moist filling is added.

1 Heat the oven to 400°F. Heat a baking sheet in the oven. Line the pastry shell with a double thickness of aluminum foil, pushing well into the bottom. Half-fill with dried beans or rice. Bake on the baking sheet until set and the rim starts to brown, about 15 minutes.

2 Remove the foil and beans or rice, and reduce the oven temperature to 375°F. Bake, 5–10 minutes longer, or as directed.

3 Transfer the pastry shell, in the plate, to a wire rack, and let cool before adding the filling.

2 MAKE THE LEMON CURD

1 Finely grate the zest from 2 of the lemons onto parchment paper. Set the zest aside.

ANNE SAYS
"Scrape off the lemon zest remaining on the grater."

Strain out lemon pulp and bitter seeds

Twist lemon on juicer to extract maximum juice

2 Halve the lemons. Squeeze the juice, and strain it into a measuring cup. There should be about 1 cup.

3 Beat the egg yolks with the whole eggs, using the whisk, until evenly mixed together. Cut the butter into small pieces.

4 Put the sugar, lemon zest, and butter into a medium heavy-based saucepan. Add the lemon juice. Whisk over fairly low heat until the sugar has dissolved, 2–3 minutes.

5 Off the heat, whisk in the beaten eggs and egg yolks until evenly combined with the lemon mixture.

6 Return to the heat and cook gently, so the curd thickens slowly and does not curdle, stirring constantly with the wooden spoon, until it is thick enough to coat the back of the spoon, 4–6 minutes.

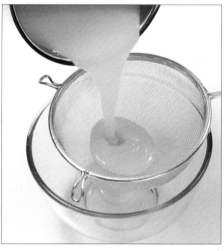

Blind-baked pastry shell will not become soggy when moist filling is added

7 Strain the lemon curd into a bowl to remove any bits of egg or lemon zest, and set aside to let cool.

8 Spoon the lemon curd into the prepared pastry shell. Bake on the baking sheet just until the mixture starts to set, 10–12 minutes. Transfer to the wire rack, and let cool, then chill until adding the meringue. The curd will set further when cold.

3 MAKE THE ITALIAN MERINGUE AND FINISH THE PIE

2 Put the egg whites into a metal bowl, and whisk with an electric mixer or by hand. Begin whisking slowly, but increase the speed when the egg whites become foamy and white. Continue whisking the egg whites until stiff peaks form when the beaters are lifted.

1 Heat the sugar and water until dissolved. Boil, without stirring, until the syrup reaches the hard-ball stage (248°F on a candy thermometer). Meanwhile, prepare to whisk the egg whites, so they are ready just when the syrup reaches hard-ball stage. To test for hard-ball stage, remove the syrup from the heat, take a small spoonful, and let cool a few seconds. Take a little syrup between forefinger and thumb. It should form a firm, pliable ball.

Egg whites reach maximum volume when whisked in metal bowl

How to Fill a Pastry Bag

Use a rubber spatula or pastry scraper when filling a pastry bag with meringue or cream.

1 Drop a tube into a pastry bag, and twist, tucking the bag into the tube. This prevents the mixture from leaking.

2 Fold the top of the bag over your hand. Add the meringue or cream to be piped, pressing it down into the bag.

3 Twist the top of the bag until no air is left in it. To pipe, hold the twisted top of the bag between thumb and forefinger, and squeeze the bag gently to press out the mixture. Do not squeeze the bag with your other hand, but use it to guide the tube as you pipe.

3 Gradually pour the hot sugar syrup into the beaten egg whites, beating constantly.

! TAKE CARE !
Be sure to pour the syrup directly into the egg whites so that it does not stick to the side of the bowl.

Damp dish towel under bowl keeps it from slipping

Beat constantly while pouring in hot sugar syrup

4 Continue beating the mixture until the meringue is cool and stiff, about 5 minutes.

5 Heat the broiler. With the metal spatula, spread half of the meringue over the filling to cover.

6 Put the remaining meringue into the pastry bag with the large star tube (see box, left). Pipe decorations like the spokes of a wheel over the pie, finishing with a rosette in the center.

Central rosette should be same height as surrounding meringue, so top browns evenly

26

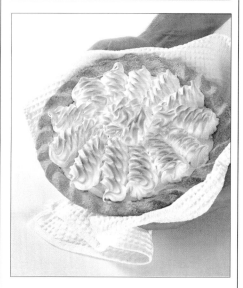

7 Broil the pie about 3 inches from the heat until the meringue is golden brown, 1–2 minutes.

ANNE SAYS
"*Make sure that you broil the meringue at once, so it does not start to separate and become sticky.*"

¶◎¶ TO SERVE
Transfer the pie to a serving platter, and serve from the pie plate, while the meringue is warm and the filling is chilled. Cut it into wedges with a knife dipped in hot water, to cut cleanly.

V A R I A T I O N

CRANBERRY MERINGUE PIE

In this colorful variation of Lemon Meringue Pie, bright red sour cranberries are simmered with sugar just until they pop and release their juices, then thickened with eggs. To add texture, the cranberry curd is left unstrained.

1 Omit the lemon curd. Make and chill the pie pastry dough; line the pie plate, scallop the pastry edge (see page 123), and blind bake the shell as directed.
2 Make the cranberry filling: beat 3 egg yolks with 3 whole eggs until mixed.

3 In a medium heavy-based saucepan, combine ³/₄ cup sugar, 2 cups fresh cranberries, and ¹/₂ cup water. Simmer, stirring occasionally, just until the cranberries pop, 5–7 minutes. Lower the heat, and stir in 2 tbsp butter. Remove from the heat, and whisk in the eggs. Continue cooking over low heat, stirring constantly with a wooden spoon, until the curd has thickened enough to coat the back of the spoon, 4–6 minutes. Let the curd cool slightly.

Fluted golden pastry edge looks appetizing

Piped broiled meringue is a mouthwatering finish

4 Spoon the cranberry curd into the pastry shell, and bake as directed. Let cool, and chill as directed.
5 Make the Italian meringue as directed. With a metal spatula, spread the meringue over the cranberry filling to cover it completely, mounding it well; then make decorative swirls in the meringue with the metal spatula. Broil and serve the pie as directed.

SPIRITED EGGNOG PIE

¶◎¶ SERVES 6–8 ⌇ WORK TIME 40–45 MINUTES* ❄ SETTING TIME 2–3 HOURS

EQUIPMENT

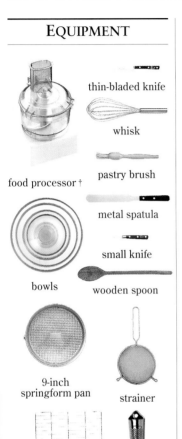

thin-bladed knife

whisk

pastry brush

food processor †

metal spatula

small knife

bowls

wooden spoon

9-inch springform pan

strainer

wire rack

small grater

baking sheet

saucepans, 1 heavy-based with lid

rubber spatula

†rolling pin and plastic bag can also be used

In this recipe, the holiday treat of eggnog is transformed into a creamy, rum-flavored pie, which is chilled, then topped with freshly grated nutmeg just before serving. The crust is made of almond-flavored Amaretti cookies, which are crushed to crumbs, then moistened with butter. Other types of crisp cookie can also be used.

GETTING AHEAD

The pie can be made up to 1 day ahead and kept, covered, in the refrigerator. Add the nutmeg just before serving.

*plus 15 minutes chilling and 10–15 minutes blind baking

INGREDIENTS

egg yolks

milk

vanilla bean

dark rum

sugar

heavy cream

Amaretti cookies

unsalted butter

powdered gelatin

whole nutmeg †

cornstarch

†¹/₄ tsp ground nutmeg can also be used

SHOPPING LIST

2 cups	milk
1	vanilla bean or 1 tsp vanilla extract
¹/₄ cup	sugar
2 tbsp	cornstarch
4	egg yolks
¹/₂ cup	heavy cream
1 tbsp	powdered gelatin
¹/₄ cup	dark rum, more to taste
	whole nutmeg for sprinkling
	For the Amaretti cookie crust
¹/₂ cup	unsalted butter, more for springform pan
¹/₂ lb	Amaretti cookies

ORDER OF WORK

1 MAKE AND BAKE THE AMARETTI COOKIE CRUST

2 MAKE THE CUSTARD

3 FINISH THE FILLING; ASSEMBLE THE PIE

1 MAKE AND BAKE THE AMARETTI COOKIE CRUST

1 Heat the oven to 350°F. Melt the butter in a small saucepan. Brush the springform pan with melted butter. Put the Amaretti cookies in the food processor, and grind them into fine crumbs. Alternatively, put the cookies in a plastic bag and crush them with a rolling pin. Transfer the Amaretti cookie crumbs to a medium bowl.

2 Add the melted butter to the crumbs, and stir until all the crumbs are moistened.

3 Press the crumb mixture evenly over the bottom and 1 inch up the side of the pan. Chill until firm, about 15 minutes. Put the baking sheet in the oven to heat. Bake the crust on the heated baking sheet, 10–15 minutes. Let cool on the wire rack.

Use back of metal spoon to press crumb mixture into pan

2 MAKE THE CUSTARD

1 Put the milk in the heavy-based saucepan. Split the vanilla bean lengthwise in half, and add it to the milk. Bring just to a boil, then remove from the heat, cover, and let stand in a warm place, 10–15 minutes. Remove the vanilla bean, rinse it, and store to use again.

2 Set aside one-quarter of the milk. Add the sugar to the remaining hot milk in the saucepan; stir until dissolved.

3 Put the cornstarch and egg yolks in a medium bowl and whisk them together until smooth.

4 Whisk the sweetened hot milk into the cornstarch and egg yolk mixture, and continue to whisk just until the custard mixture is smooth.

Pour sweetened milk in steady stream

5 Pour the mixture back into the heavy-based saucepan, and cook over medium heat, stirring constantly with the wooden spoon, just until it comes to a boil and is thick enough to coat the back of the spoon. Your finger will leave a clear trail across the back of the spoon.

! TAKE CARE !
Do not continue to boil the custard, or it may curdle.

Stir in figure-of-eight motion, so custard does not scorch on bottom of pan

Bring custard just to a boil to cook egg yolks

6 Off the heat, stir the reserved milk into the custard, and strain it into a cold bowl. Stir in the vanilla extract, if using. Cover tightly to prevent a skin from forming on the surface of the custard, and let cool to tepid.

3 FINISH THE FILLING; ASSEMBLE THE PIE

1 Pour the cream into a chilled bowl, and whip with the whisk until soft peaks form; cover, and chill.

2 Sprinkle the gelatin evenly over the rum in a small saucepan. Let soak, 5 minutes. The gelatin will soften to a spongy consistency. Set pan over low heat, and melt until pourable, shaking the pan occasionally, 1–2 minutes.

! TAKE CARE !
Do not stir the gelatin, or it will cook into strings or form lumps.

3 Stir the gelatin mixture into the tepid custard. Taste the custard, adding more rum, if you like.

Stir melted gelatin into warm custard, so they mix evenly

4 Set the bowl of custard in a larger bowl half-filled with ice water, and stir gently until the custard starts to thicken and set.

5 Remove the bowl of setting custard immediately from the bowl of ice water and whisk the custard briskly to lighten it, about 10 seconds.

6 Add the whipped cream to the custard, and fold together gently, scooping under the custard and turning the mixture over. At the same time, turn bowl counter-clockwise.

7 Pour the filling into the cookie crust, smooth the top with the metal spatula, if necessary, then chill the pie until set, 2–3 hours.

⦿ TO SERVE

Run the thin-bladed knife around the inside of the pan; loosen and remove the side. Grate nutmeg over the filling, or sprinkle with ground nutmeg. Transfer the pie to a serving plate and serve chilled. Use a knife dipped in hot water to cut the pie into wedges.

Sprinkling of nutmeg is traditional topping for eggnog and complements rum in filling

Amaretti cookie crust surrounds creamy custard

IRISH COFFEE TARTLETS

Coffee and Irish whiskey flavor the custard in this variation, mimicking the beverage that is renowned in Ireland and internationally.

1 Omit the nutmeg, vanilla, and rum. Make double the quantity of the Amaretti cookie crust, using 1 cup unsalted butter and 1 lb Amaretti cookies. Press the mixture into eight 4-inch tartlet pans with removable bases, and chill and bake as directed, 8–10 minutes.

2 Make the custard: put the milk in a heavy-based saucepan with 3 tbsp instant coffee granules and bring just to a boil, stirring until the coffee is dissolved. Finish the custard as directed. Finish the filling, using whiskey in place of rum. Assemble tartlets as directed. Chill until set, 2–3 hours.

3 Meanwhile, make Chantilly cream to decorate the tartlets: pour $3/4$ cup heavy cream into a chilled bowl; whip until soft peaks form. Add 2 tsp confectioners' sugar, and $1/2$ tsp vanilla extract, and continue whipping until stiff peaks form. Chill until ready to use.

4 Put the Chantilly cream into a pastry bag fitted with a star tube, and pipe a cream rosette on top of each tartlet. Decorate with brown sugar crystals, if you like. Serve within 2 hours.

Double-Crust Rhubarb and Strawberry Pie

🍽 Serves 6–8　🥣 Work Time 30–35 minutes*　🍲 Baking Time 50–55 minutes

Equipment

pastry brush

chef's knife

9-inch pie plate

small knife

grater

large metal spoon

chopping board

bowls

parchment paper

rolling pin

strainer

aluminum foil

metal skewer

baking sheet

wire rack

Tart rhubarb, the first fruit of spring, is united with sweet strawberries in this double-crusted American favorite, which is good warm or at room temperature. So popular is rhubarb in pies that it is often called the pie plant.

Getting Ahead

The pie pastry dough can be made up to 2 days ahead and kept, tightly wrapped, in the refrigerator. The pie is best the day it is baked.

plus 1 hour chilling time

Ingredients

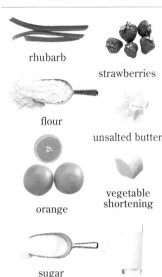

rhubarb

strawberries

flour

unsalted butter

orange

vegetable shortening

sugar

milk

Shopping List

2 lb	rhubarb
1½ pints	strawberries
1	orange
1¼ cups	sugar
¼ tsp	salt
¼ cup	flour
1 tbsp	unsalted butter, more for pie plate
	For the pie pastry dough
2½ cups	flour
2 tbsp	sugar (optional)
½ tsp	salt
¾ cup	vegetable shortening
6–7 tbsp	cold water, more if needed
	For the glaze
1 tbsp	milk
1 tbsp	sugar

Order of Work

1　Make the Pie Pastry Dough and Line the Pie Plate

2　Prepare the Fruit Filling and Fill the Prepared Pastry Shell

3　Cover, Decorate, and Bake the Pie

1 MAKE THE PIE PASTRY DOUGH AND LINE THE PIE PLATE

Use quick strokes of knife to trim dough shell

1 Make and chill the dough (see box, page 69), adding the sugar, if using, with the flour. Brush the pie plate with melted butter. Lightly flour the work surface. Roll out two-thirds of the dough into a round 2 inches larger than the top of the pie plate. Using the rolling pin, drape the dough over the pie plate.

2 Gently lift the edge of the dough with the fingertips of one hand, and press it well into the bottom and up the side of the pie plate with the fingertips of the other hand.

3 Lift the plate, and trim the dough even with the outer edge of the plate, using a table knife. Reserve the trimmings. Chill the pastry shell until firm, about 15 minutes.

2 PREPARE THE FRUIT FILLING AND FILL THE PREPARED PASTRY SHELL

1 Trim the rhubarb stalks, wash, then drain them. Gather 2 or 3 stalks together at a time, and cut crosswise into ½-inch slices. Hull the strawberries, washing only if dirty. Halve or quarter them according to size.

Look for bright red crisp stalks when buying rhubarb

2 Using the medium grid of the grater, grate the zest from the orange onto a piece of parchment paper.

3 In a bowl, combine the rhubarb, orange zest, sugar, salt, and flour, and stir to mix. Add the strawberries and toss gently.

4 Spoon the fruit mixture into the lined pie plate, doming it slightly. Cut the butter into small pieces and dot the pieces over the filling.

Cubes of butter enrich filling

3 COVER, DECORATE, AND BAKE THE PIE

1 Brush the edge of the pastry shell with cold water. Roll out the remaining dough into an 11-inch round. Wrap it around the rolling pin and drape it over the filling.

Drape dough over filling without stretching it

Edge of pastry shell is brushed with water so top crust will stick to it

2 With the small knife, trim the top crust even with the bottom crust. Press the edges together to seal them.

3 Make a pastry rose with the dough trimmings (see box, below). Brush a little cold water onto the center of the top crust, and press the rose on top.

4 With the small knife, cut steam vents around the top crust of the pie.

HOW TO MAKE A PASTRY ROSE

A pastry rose is a traditional decoration for sweet and savory pies with a top crust. Simple to make with dough trimmings, it gives an effective finish to a pie.

1 Roll out dough into a 3- x 12-inch rectangle, ¼-inch thick. Flour the dough; cut into 4 squares. Stack the squares.

2 Balance the squares on one forefinger. Pull the corners downward, and squeeze the layers in the other hand to make a ball.

3 With a small knife, and without cutting through to the base, cut a deep cross in the smooth upper surface of the ball of dough.

4 Open out the layers of dough to form the rose petals. Cut off and discard the dough from the base of the rose.

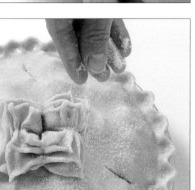

5 Scallop the edge of the pie: place the forefinger of one hand on the edge of the dough, pointing outward. With the forefinger and thumb of your other hand, push dough inward to form a scallop. Repeat around the pie.

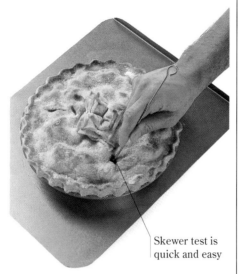

Skewer test is quick and easy

6 Brush the top crust with the milk, and sprinkle with the sugar. Chill until firm, about 15 minutes. Heat the oven to 425°F. Put the baking sheet in the oven to heat.

7 Bake the pie on the baking sheet in the heated oven, 20 minutes. Reduce the oven temperature to 350°F, and continue baking until the rhubarb is tender when pierced with the skewer through a steam vent, and the crust is browned, 30–35 minutes longer. Transfer to the wire rack, and let cool.

🍽 TO SERVE
Transfer the pie plate to a serving platter. Cut the pie into wedges, and serve warm, or at room temperature.

Golden pastry rose is pretty finishing touch

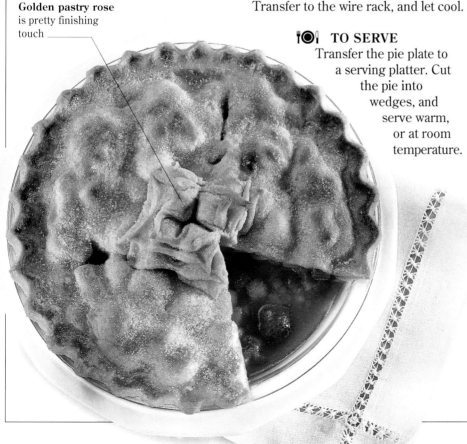

V A R I A T I O N

DOUBLE-CRUST APPLE PIE

Serve this classic pie hot, with a slice of Cheddar cheese, or with a scoop of ice cream.

1 Omit the rhubarb, strawberries, and orange. Make and chill the pie pastry dough, and line the pie plate as directed. Chill the shell as directed.
2 Peel 2 lb firm tart apples; then cut out the flower and stem ends. Halve the apples, and scoop out the cores. Set each apple half, cut-side down, on a chopping board, and cut crosswise into medium slices. Transfer to a bowl. Sprinkle with the juice of 1 lemon.
3 Sprinkle $\frac{1}{2}$ cup sugar, 2 tbsp flour, $\frac{1}{2}$ tsp ground cinnamon, $\frac{1}{4}$ tsp ground nutmeg, and a pinch of salt over the apples. Toss until coated. Taste the apples, adding more sugar or spice, if you like. Spoon into the lined pie plate.
4 Roll out the remaining dough, and cover the pie as directed. With a small knife, cut an "x" in the center of the top crust. Gently pull back the point of each triangle to reveal the filling. Scallop the edge as directed, but push inward at an angle, to make a sharper scallop.
5 Roll out the dough trimmings into a narrow 20-inch strip. Cut it lengthwise into two $\frac{1}{8}$-inch strips. Brush the top crust with a little cold water, and lay the strips in a wavy criss-cross pattern around it. Finish and bake the pie as directed. Serve hot.

LEMON TART

Tarte au Citron

🍽️ SERVES 8   🥣 WORK TIME 40–45 MINUTES*   🍲 BAKING TIME 25–30 MINUTES**

EQUIPMENT

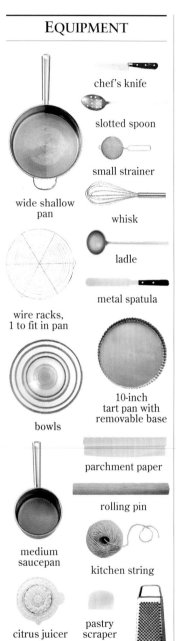

- chef's knife
- slotted spoon
- small strainer
- wide shallow pan
- whisk
- ladle
- metal spatula
- wire racks, 1 to fit in pan
- bowls
- 10-inch tart pan with removable base
- parchment paper
- rolling pin
- medium saucepan
- kitchen string
- citrus juicer
- pastry scraper
- grater
- aluminum foil
- kitchen scissors
- baking sheet
- rice

This recipe, with a filling of citrus zest and juice in a smooth custard, is the inspiration of Maurice Ferré from Maxim's restaurant in Paris.

GETTING AHEAD

Candy the lemon slices at least 1 day, and up to 2 days, ahead, and keep them at room temperature. The dough can be made up to 1 day ahead and kept, tightly wrapped, in the refrigerator. Bake the tart not more than 8 hours in advance, and add the candied lemon slices just before serving.

*plus 45 minutes chilling and 24 hours standing
**plus 15 minutes blind baking

SHOPPING LIST

1	orange
3	lemons
3	eggs
1	egg yolk
³⁄₄ cup	sugar
	For the candied lemon slices
2	lemons
1¹⁄₄ cups	sugar
2 cups	water
	For the pâte sucrée dough
1¹⁄₂ cups	flour, more if needed
6 tbsp	unsalted butter, more for tart pan
¹⁄₃ cup	sugar
¹⁄₂ tsp	vanilla extract
¹⁄₄ tsp	salt
3	egg yolks

INGREDIENTS

- lemons
- orange
- egg yolks
- sugar
- flour
- eggs
- vanilla extract
- unsalted butter

ANNE SAYS

"The lemon slices must be candied at least 1 day ahead, so if you are short of time, you can omit them, and decorate the tart instead with rosettes of Chantilly cream."

ORDER OF WORK

1 CANDY THE LEMON SLICES

2 MAKE THE DOUGH, LINE THE TART PAN, AND BLIND BAKE THE PASTRY SHELL

3 MAKE THE FILLING; FILL AND FINISH THE TART

1 CANDY THE LEMON SLICES

1 Trim off and discard the ends from the lemons. Cut each lemon into ⅛-inch slices; discard any seeds.

2 Bring a medium saucepan of water to a boil. Add the lemon slices, and simmer to blanch the slices just until they begin to soften, about 3 minutes. With the slotted spoon, remove a few lemon slices at a time. Let drain.

Lemon slices should be just covered with water

4 Bring the syrup slowly to a simmer, taking 10–12 minutes. Poach the lemon slices until tender to the bite, about 1 hour. Add more water during cooking, if necessary, so the slices are always covered. Take the pan from the heat, and let the candied lemon slices cool in the syrup. Let stand in the syrup, covered with the paper round, at room temperature, 24 hours.

3 Attach 3 lengths of kitchen string to an upturned round wire rack. Heat the sugar and water in the wide shallow pan until dissolved, then bring just to a boil. Put the lemon slices on the rack, tie the strings together, and lower into the syrup. Press a round of parchment paper on top.

String handle makes lowering and lifting rack from pan easy

2 MAKE THE DOUGH, LINE THE TART PAN, AND BLIND BAKE THE PASTRY SHELL

1 Make and chill the dough (see box, page 18). Brush the pan with melted butter. Lightly flour the work surface; roll out the chilled dough into a 12-inch round. Wrap it around the rolling pin and drape it over the pan.

2 Gently lift the edge of the dough with one hand, and press it into the bottom of the pan with the other hand. Overlap the dough slightly inside the pan rim. Roll the rolling pin over the top of the pan to cut off excess dough.

3 With your thumbs, press the dough evenly up the side of the tart pan, from the bottom edge, to increase the height of the pastry rim. Chill the pastry shell until it is firm, about 15 minutes.

4 Heat the oven to 400°F. Put the baking sheet in the oven to heat. Line the pastry shell with a double thickness of foil. Half-fill with rice.

5 Bake the pastry shell on the baking sheet in the heated oven until set and the rim starts to brown, about 10 minutes. Remove foil and rice. Reduce oven temperature to 375°F. Continue baking until pale brown, about 5 minutes longer. Leave the oven on. Transfer the shell in the pan to a wire rack. Let cool slightly.

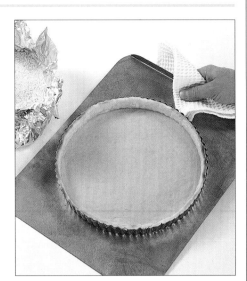

3 MAKE THE FILLING; FILL AND FINISH THE TART

Orange juice mellows tartness of lemon juice

1 Grate the zest from the orange and lemons, then squeeze the fruit and strain the juice. There should be 1 cup.

Colored zest should be grated without any bitter white pith

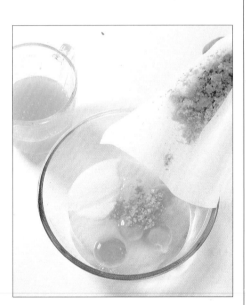

2 Put the eggs, egg yolk, and sugar in a medium bowl. Add the orange and lemon zest and juice, and whisk together until thoroughly combined.

3 Set the pastry shell on the baking sheet. Ladle the filling into the pastry shell, then bake in the heated oven until set, 25–30 minutes.

4 Transfer the tart to the wire rack, and let cool slightly. Set the tart on a bowl to loosen and remove the side.

Side of tart pan slips off easily

5 Slide the tart from the pan base onto a flat platter, and let cool to room temperature. Lift the rack of candied lemon slices out of the syrup and drain, 1–2 minutes.

6 Using the metal spatula, arrange the candied lemon slices over the filling, starting at the edge. Serve, cut into wedges.

Candied lemon slices finish the tart

VARIATION
LIME AND CARDAMOM TART
This tart, with its smooth and creamy lime custard filling, is topped with piped Chantilly cream and lime julienne.

1 Substitute 4 limes for 4 of the lemons; omit the sugar and water for candying. Make and chill dough, line pan, and blind bake shell as directed.
2 Pare the zest from 1 lime. Cut into very fine julienne strips. Bring a small saucepan of water to a boil, add the zest strips, and simmer to blanch, 2–3 minutes. Drain, rinse in cold water, and drain again thoroughly.
3 Grate the zest from 2 of the remaining limes and from the lemon, then squeeze the juice from the lemon and all 4 limes; there should be ³/₄ cup juice. Make the filling as directed, using the lime and lemon juice and zest, and adding ²/₃ cup heavy cream, and ¹/₂ tsp ground cardamom. Bake, cool, and unmold the tart as directed.
4 Make the Chantilly cream (see box, right), using 1 cup heavy cream, ¹/₂ tsp vanilla extract, and 2–3 tsp confectioners' sugar. Put the cream into a pastry bag fitted with a medium star tube; pipe cream over the tart. Sprinkle edge with the lime julienne, and serve as directed.

HOW TO MAKE CHANTILLY CREAM

1 Pour heavy cream into a chilled bowl. Whip with a whisk or electric mixer until it forms soft peaks. Add flavoring and sugar; whip until the cream forms soft peaks again and just holds its shape.

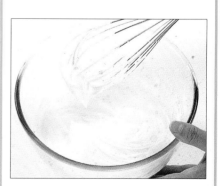

2 Continue whipping until the cream forms stiff peaks and the whisk leaves clear marks. Do not overwhip or it will separate.

PEAR PIE WITH WALNUT PASTRY

Le Poirat

 SERVES 6–8 WORK TIME 35–40 MINUTES* BAKING TIME 35–40 MINUTES

EQUIPMENT

9-inch tart pan with removable base

food processor †

chef's knife

small knife

strainer

vegetable peeler

pastry brush

peppermill

pastry scraper

2¹/₂-inch cookie cutter

bowls

wire rack

baking sheet

chopping board

rolling pin

citrus juicer

metal skewer

† rotary cheese grater can also be used

In this specialty from central France, wedges of pear are sandwiched between a double crust of walnut pastry. Serve the pie warm, accompanied with crème fraîche or whipped heavy cream.

GETTING AHEAD

The walnut pastry dough can be made up to 2 days ahead and kept, tightly wrapped, in the refrigerator. The pie is best served the day of baking, but it can be stored in an airtight container, up to 1 day. Warm it in a low oven and add the crème fraîche just before serving.

plus 2 ¹/₄ hours chilling time

SHOPPING LIST

1	lemon
1³/₄ lb	pears
¹/₂ tsp	freshly ground black pepper
1 tbsp	sugar
1¹/₂ cups	crème fraîche (see box, page 44) for serving (optional)
	For the walnut pastry dough
¹/₂ cup	walnut pieces
²/₃ cup	sugar
2 cups	flour, more if needed
²/₃ cup	unsalted butter, more for tart pan
1	egg
¹/₂ tsp	salt
1 tsp	ground cinnamon

INGREDIENTS

walnut pieces

pears

lemon

unsalted butter

sugar

ground cinnamon

black peppercorns

flour

egg

ANNE SAYS

"Crème fraîche is easy but time-consuming to make. You can buy it at some supermarkets, or use whipped heavy cream instead."

ORDER OF WORK

1 MAKE THE WALNUT PASTRY DOUGH

2 ROLL OUT THE WALNUT PASTRY DOUGH AND LINE THE TART PAN

3 FILL, COVER, AND BAKE THE PIE

MAKE THE WALNUT PASTRY DOUGH

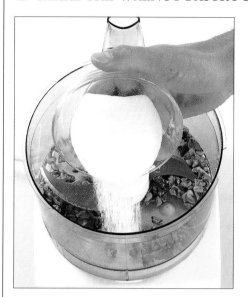

1 Put the walnut pieces in the food processor. Add about half of the sugar, and finely grind. Alternatively, grind the walnuts in a rotary cheese grater, then mix with half of the sugar.

ANNE SAYS
"The sugar helps keep the walnuts from becoming oily in the food processor."

2 Sift the flour onto the work surface, add the ground walnut and sugar mixture, then make a large well in the center of the ingredients. Using the rolling pin, pound the butter to soften it slightly.

Dough will be moist enough to come together easily when worked with your fingers

3 Put the egg, the remaining sugar, the butter, salt, and ground cinnamon into the well. With your fingertips, work the ingredients in the well until they are all thoroughly mixed together.

4 Draw in the flour with the pastry scraper, then work the flour into the other ingredients with your fingers until coarse crumbs form.

6 Sprinkle the work surface lightly with flour. Blend the dough by pushing it away from you with the heel of your hand. Gather up the dough and continue to blend in this manner until it is very smooth and peels away from the work surface in one piece, 1–2 minutes. Shape into a smooth ball, wrap tightly, and chill until firm, 1 hour.

Knead thoroughly to combine flour and butter so dough is very pliable

5 Press the dough into a ball. It should be quite soft, but if it is too sticky, add a little more flour.

Flour work surface sparingly because too much added flour can toughen dough

2 ROLL OUT THE WALNUT PASTRY DOUGH AND LINE THE TART PAN

1 Brush the tart pan with melted butter. Lightly flour the work surface. Roll out two-thirds of the chilled dough into an 11-inch round. Rewrap and return the unrolled dough to the refrigerator.

Apply even pressure to rolling pin

2 Wrap the dough around the rolling pin. Gently drape it over the pan.

3 Lift edge of dough with one hand and press it into the bottom of the pan with the other hand. Overlap the dough slightly inside the rim of the pan, so extra dough is left at the edge.

4 Roll the rolling pin over the top of the pan, pressing down to cut off the excess dough. Add the trimmings to the reserved portion of dough and return to the refrigerator.

5 With your thumbs, press the dough evenly up the pan side to increase the height of the shell. Chill the shell until very firm, about 1 hour. Meanwhile, prepare the pears.

3 FILL, COVER, AND BAKE THE PIE

1 Squeeze the juice from the lemon. Peel the pears with the vegetable peeler, from stem to flower ends.

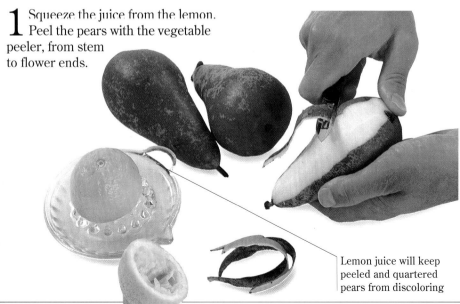

Lemon juice will keep peeled and quartered pears from discoloring

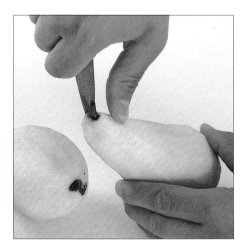

2 Using the tip of the small knife, cut out the stem and flower ends from each pear.

3 Cut each pear into quarters, then scoop out the central stems and cores with the small knife.

4 Put the pear wedges into a medium bowl. Grind the black pepper over them, and add the lemon juice. Toss until the pears are coated.

5 Shaking off any excess lemon juice, arrange the pear wedges evenly in a cartwheel pattern on the bottom of the pastry shell.

Quartered pears fit neatly in pastry shell

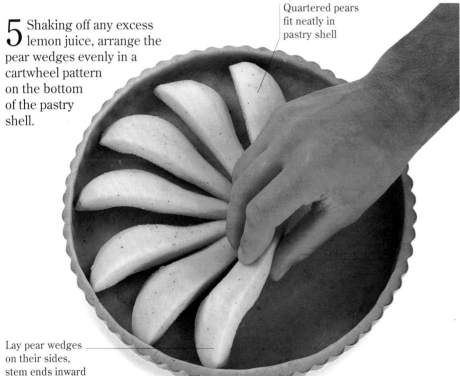

Lay pear wedges on their sides, stem ends inward

6 Roll out the remaining dough into a 10-inch round; stamp out a 2½-inch round from the center, using the cookie cutter.

ANNE SAYS
"You can also use a glass to stamp out the round."

7 Wrap the dough around the rolling pin, and drape it carefully over the pear wedges.

Hold knife vertically to trim dough neatly

Use tart pan as your guide to trim top crust

8 With the small knife, trim the top round even with the filled pastry shell, using the pan as a guide.

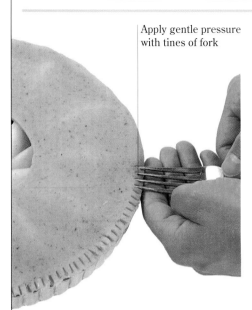

Apply gentle pressure with tines of fork

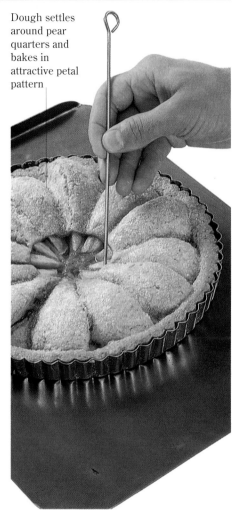

Dough settles around pear quarters and bakes in attractive petal pattern

9 Press the dough edges together with the back of a fork to seal the top and bottom of the pastry shell.

10 Brush the top with water, and sprinkle with the sugar. Chill the pie until firm, about 15 minutes. Heat the oven to 375°F. Put the baking sheet in the oven to heat.

11 Put the chilled pear pie on the baking sheet and bake in the heated oven until the pastry is browned, and the pears are tender when pierced with the metal skewer, 35–40 minutes.

CREME FRAICHE

When unpasteurized cream is left to stand, it develops a full, slightly sour taste. This is crème fraîche, the cream most frequently used in France. Modern production methods use recultured pasteurized cream. This recipe is my own homemade version of crème fraîche.

🍽 MAKES 1½ CUPS

⏱ WORK TIME 12–15 MINUTES

STANDING TIME 6–8 HOURS

SHOPPING LIST

1 cup	heavy cream
½ cup	active culture buttermilk, or sour cream plus ½ tsp lemon juice

1 Pour the cream into a medium saucepan, and add the buttermilk. Alternatively, add the sour cream and lemon juice. Stir to mix. Heat gently until barely warm (75°F). Pour the mixture into a glass bowl.

2 Cover, leaving a gap for air. Leave at room temperature (70°F), until the cream has thickened enough to hold the mark of a spoon and tastes slightly acidic, 6–8 hours. Stir, cover, and chill.

VARIATION

PEACH PIE WITH WALNUT PASTRY

When fresh summer peaches are ripe, I like to bake them in this variation of Pear Pie with Walnut Pastry, and serve the pie with ice cream.

12 Let the pie cool slightly, then while it is still warm, set the tart pan on a bowl to loosen and remove the side. Slide the pie from the pan base onto a serving plate.

⏥ TO SERVE

Cut the warm pie into wedges, and transfer to individual plates. Accompany each serving with a generous spoonful of crème fraîche, if using, and serve at once. Serve the remaining crème fraîche in a separate bowl.

1 Omit the pears and freshly ground black pepper. Make and chill the walnut pastry dough, line the tart pan, and chill the pastry shell as directed.
2 Scald, pit, and peel 1½ lb peaches: bring a saucepan of water to a boil. Immerse the peaches in the water, 10 seconds, then transfer them with a slotted spoon to a bowl of cold water.

3 With a small knife, cut 1 peach in half, using the indentation on one side as a guide. Twist with both hands to loosen the peach halves from the pit, and pull them apart. If the peach clings, loosen the flesh from the pit with a small knife. Scoop out the pit with the tip of the knife, and discard it. Repeat for the rest of the peaches. Peel the skin from the peach halves, and cut each half into 2–3 wedges. Toss the peaches with the lemon juice.
4 Arrange the peaches in the pastry shell. Cover, bake, and finish the pie as directed.
5 Cut the warm pie into wedges, and serve at once. Accompany with scoops of vanilla ice cream, served separately, if you like.

Sweet walnut dough bakes brown and crisp

Crème fraîche perfectly complements this tart

CHOCOLATE PYE WITH A CRUNCHY CRUST

 SERVES 8 WORK TIME 30–35 MINUTES* BAKING TIME 15–20 MINUTES**

EQUIPMENT

chef's knife

pastry brush

10-inch
tart pan with
removable base

bowls

food processor†

whisk

wooden spoon

rose leaves

wire rack

baking sheet

saucepans

rubber spatula

rolling pin

chopping board

†rotary cheese grater can also be
used

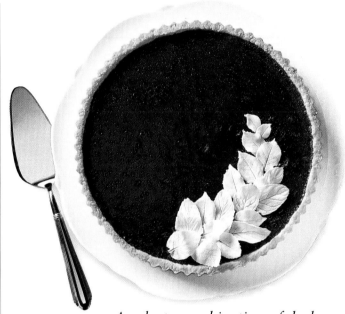

*A velvety combination of dark
chocolate and cream fills a crisp
almond crust. Although the pastry for this
attractive "pye" dates back to eighteenth-century
England, the decoration follows a modern style.*

GETTING AHEAD

The crunchy crust can be made up to 1 day ahead and kept,
tightly wrapped, in the refrigerator. The tart can be baked
1 day in advance. Keep it, covered, in the refrigerator and
allow it to come to room temperature before serving.

*plus 45 minutes chilling
**plus 8–10 minutes blind baking

SHOPPING LIST

9 oz	semisweet chocolate
1½ cups	heavy cream
2	eggs
1	egg yolk
	For the crunchy crust
⅓ cup	sugar
1½ cups	blanched almonds
1	egg white
	butter for tart pan
	For the decoration
3 oz	white chocolate

INGREDIENTS

semisweet
chocolate

heavy
cream

egg yolk

eggs

sugar

butter

blanched
almonds

egg white

white chocolate

ORDER OF WORK

1 MAKE THE
CRUNCHY CRUST

2 LINE THE PAN;
BLIND BAKE THE
CRUNCHY CRUST

3 MAKE THE
FILLING AND
DECORATION AND
FINISH THE TART

1 MAKE THE CRUNCHY CRUST

1 Put the sugar and blanched almonds in the food processor, and finely grind them. Alternatively, grind just the almonds in a rotary cheese grater, then stir in the sugar.

ANNE SAYS
"The sugar helps keep the blanched almonds from becoming oily in the food processor."

2 In a medium bowl, whisk the egg white just until it is frothy.

3 Transfer the ground almond and sugar mixture from the food processor to the beaten egg white.

Mixture comes together easily with help of wooden spoon

4 Stir the mixture with the wooden spoon to form a stiff paste. Shape it into a ball, wrap tightly, and chill until firm, about 30 minutes.

2 LINE THE PAN; BLIND BAKE THE CRUNCHY CRUST

1 Melt a little butter in a small saucepan, then brush the tart pan with the melted butter.

Rolling pin is ideal for flattening dough

2 Lightly flour the work surface, then lightly pound or press out the dough with the rolling pin to flatten it.

Almonds, sugar, and egg white will make deliciously crunchy crust

3 Transfer the dough to the tart pan. With the back of a spoon, dipped into cold water, or with the heel of your hand, press the dough into the bottom of the pan, then push it well up the side. Chill until firm, about 15 minutes.

Dough is easy to spread when spoon is dipped in cold water

4 Heat the oven to 350°F. Put the baking sheet in the oven to heat. Put the shell on the baking sheet, and bake in the heated oven until lightly browned, 8–10 minutes. Slide the shell off the baking sheet, onto the wire rack. Let cool. Leave the oven on while you are making the filling for the tart.

HOW TO CHOP CHOCOLATE

If necessary, chill chocolate before chopping. Use a dry chopping board, because moisture can affect melting. Work quickly to keep chocolate from melting on the board.

1 Put the chocolate on a chopping board. With a chef's knife, cut the chocolate into small chunks.

2 To chop by hand: With broad end of knife, chop until fine. Rock handle up and down, holding tip down with the heel of other hand.

Rocking action makes it quick and easy to chop chocolate

3 To chop in a food processor: Put the chocolate chunks into a food processor, then chop, using the pulse button. If necessary, chop the chunks in several batches.

! TAKE CARE !
Do not overwork the chocolate or the heat of the machine may melt it.

3 MAKE THE FILLING AND DECORATION AND FINISH THE TART

1 Chop the semisweet chocolate (see box, page 48), and put it into a medium bowl. In a saucepan, bring the cream just to a boil. Pour the cream over the chocolate.

2 Whisk the chocolate and cream together until the chocolate has melted completely. Set the mixture aside to cool to tepid.

When chocolate melts in hot cream, mixture will darken in color

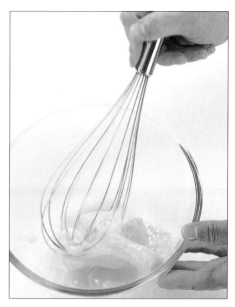

3 Put the eggs and the egg yolk into another bowl, and whisk them together until mixed.

4 Whisk the tepid chocolate and cream mixture into the beaten eggs just to combine.

5 Carefully pour the filling into the cooled shell. Put the tart on the baking sheet, and bake in the heated oven until the filling begins to set, but is still soft in center, 15–20 minutes.

Filling is smooth and rich

6 Let the tart cool slightly on the wire rack, then carefully loosen the pastry from the side of the pan. Set the tart pan on a bowl, and remove the side. Slide the tart from the pan base onto the wire rack to cool thoroughly.

ANNE SAYS
"Here, ganache, a mixture of boiled heavy cream and melted chocolate, is combined with eggs to make chocolate custard to fill the tart."

HOW TO MAKE CHOCOLATE LEAVES

White and semisweet chocolate facsimiles can be made of pliable leaves with deep veins, such as rose leaves. Chocolate leaves can be layered with parchment paper, then stored in the refrigerator, up to 1 week.

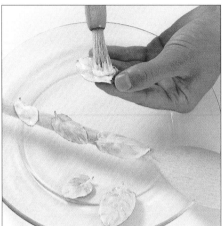

1 Put the chopped chocolate in a small bowl set over a saucepan half-filled with hot water. Heat very gently, stirring occasionally with a wooden spoon, just until the chocolate has melted, 2–3 minutes.

2 Using a pastry brush, spread the chocolate on the underside of each leaf in a thin, even layer, leaving a little of the stem exposed. Drape some leaves on the handle of a wooden spoon so they curl; set the rest on a plate to cool flat. Chill until set.

3 With the tips of your thumb and forefinger, peel away each rose leaf from the chocolate, handling as little as possible so the chocolate does not melt and become dull.

Moist chocolate filling is delicious set in crispy almond crust

7 Meanwhile, chop the white chocolate in the same way as the semisweet chocolate (see box, page 48), and use to make 15–20 chocolate leaves (see box, above). Transfer the tart to a serving plate, and decorate with the chocolate leaves.

¶Ⓞ¶ TO SERVE
Serve the chocolate tart at room temperature, cut into wedges.

VARIATION
CHOCOLATE AND CHESTNUT PYE WITH A CRUNCHY CRUST

Mixed in this chocolate tart, chestnuts are a real treat. Sumptuous chocolate curls make the perfect finishing touch.

1 Make the crunchy crust, line the tart pan, and blind bake the shell as directed in the main recipe.
2 Lightly crush 6 oz peeled canned or vacuum-packed chestnuts. Sprinkle the crushed chestnuts evenly over the bottom of the shell.
3 Make the chocolate filling, pour it over the chestnuts, and bake the tart as directed. Let cool.
4 Omit the white chocolate decoration. Make long chocolate curls: melt 3 oz semisweet chocolate as for the white chocolate. With a metal spatula, spread the melted chocolate on a baking sheet in an even, thin layer. Leave until the chocolate has just set, 15–20 minutes. Holding a chef's knife or a metal spatula at a 45° angle, push the blade away from you across the chocolate to form long curls.

5 Arrange the chocolate curls in a spoke pattern on top of the tart; dust with 1 tbsp cocoa powder.
6 Transfer the tart to a serving plate. Serve the tart at room temperature, cut into wedges.

VARIATION
CHOCOLATE MINT PYE WITH A CRUNCHY CRUST

Crushed fresh mint infuses the heavy cream to add a refreshing flavor to the filling in this version of Chocolate Pye with a Crunchy Crust, and the white chocolate decoration is piped.

1 Make the crunchy crust, line the tart pan, and blind bake the shell as directed in the main recipe.
2 Rinse 1 large bunch of fresh mint (about 2 oz). Reserve 8 small sprigs of mint for decoration. Put the remaining mint sprigs in a medium saucepan and lightly crush them, using the end of a rolling pin.
3 Pour the heavy cream over the crushed mint, and bring just to a boil. Remove from the heat, cover, and set aside to infuse, 10–15 minutes.
4 Chop the semisweet chocolate as directed, and place in a bowl. Bring the cream just back to a boil, then strain it into the bowl of chopped chocolate. Finish the filling, and bake the tart as directed.

5 Snip off a corner from the bottom of a small plastic bag to use as a pastry bag for piping the white chocolate decoration. Melt the white chocolate as directed, and spoon it into the prepared plastic bag. Pipe the melted chocolate decoratively over the tart, and leave until firm. Serve the tart at room temperature, cut into wedges, and decorate each serving with a reserved mint sprig.

STRAWBERRY MOUSSE PIE

🍽 SERVES 6–8 🥄 WORK TIME 40–45 MINUTES* ❄ SETTING TIME 1–2 HOURS

EQUIPMENT

food processor †

small knife

pastry brush

9-inch pie plate

electric mixer

saucepans, 1 heavy-based

strainer

whisk

wire rack

bowls

rolling pin

pastry scraper

aluminum foil

dried beans ‡

chopping board

baking sheet

rubber spatula

† chef's knife can also be used
‡ rice can also be used

A cross between mousse and soufflé, the strawberry and cream filling in this pie is lightly set with a small amount of gelatin. Traditionally called Bavarian creams, mixtures like these are often used in charlottes and molded desserts.

GETTING AHEAD

The dough can be made up to 2 days ahead and kept, tightly wrapped, in the refrigerator. Though best on the day of baking, when the mousse is fresh, the pie can be assembled up to 1 day ahead and kept, covered, in the refrigerator.

*plus 45 minutes chilling and 17–25 minutes blind baking

SHOPPING LIST

1 quart	strawberries
1 cup	heavy cream
2 tsp	powdered gelatin
2 tbsp	water
1/2 cup	sugar
2	egg yolks
8	sprigs of fresh mint
	For the chocolate pastry dough
1 1/4 cups	flour, more if needed
2 tbsp	cocoa powder
6 tbsp	unsalted butter, more for pie plate
3	egg yolks
1/3 cup	sugar
1/4 tsp	salt
1/2 tsp	vanilla extract

INGREDIENTS

strawberries   heavy cream

unsalted butter   cocoa powder

egg yolks   flour

powdered gelatin   sugar

fresh mint   vanilla extract

ANNE SAYS
"The filling can be made with other fruit purées, but I like to use strawberries because the pale pink of the mousse offsets the dark chocolate crust."

ORDER OF WORK

1 MAKE THE CHOCOLATE PASTRY DOUGH

2 LINE THE PLATE AND BLIND BAKE THE PASTRY SHELL

3 MAKE THE FILLING AND FINISH THE PIE

1 MAKE THE CHOCOLATE PASTRY DOUGH

1 Sift the flour and cocoa powder onto the work surface and make a large well in the center.

Pound butter lightly, so it is softened but not sticky

2 Pound the butter with the rolling pin to soften it, so that it blends in easily when it is added to the remaining dough ingredients.

Cocoa gives color as well as flavor to dough

3 Put the egg yolks, sugar, salt, vanilla extract, and softened butter into the well.

Softened butter blends easily with sugar

5 Gradually draw in the flour and cocoa powder with the pastry scraper, working them into the other ingredients with your fingertips.

4 Using your fingertips, work all the ingredients in the well together until thoroughly mixed.

Mix ingredients in well with fingertips of one hand

6 Continue working the ingredients with your fingertips until coarse crumbs form. Press the dough into a ball. If the dough is sticky, work in a little more flour.

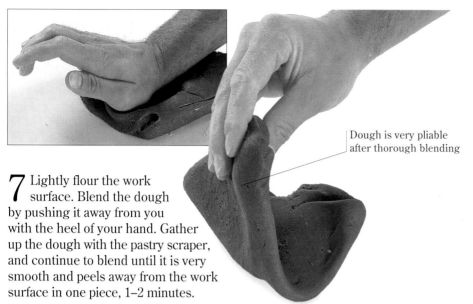

Dough is very pliable after thorough blending

7 Lightly flour the work surface. Blend the dough by pushing it away from you with the heel of your hand. Gather up the dough with the pastry scraper, and continue to blend until it is very smooth and peels away from the work surface in one piece, 1–2 minutes.

8 Shape the dough into a ball again, wrap it tightly, and chill until firm, about 30 minutes.

2 LINE THE PLATE AND BLIND BAKE THE PASTRY SHELL

1 Brush the pie plate with melted butter. Lightly flour the work surface, and roll out the chilled dough to a round 2 inches larger than the top of the pie plate. Wrap the dough around the rolling pin and drape it over the plate.

2 Gently lift the edge of the dough with the fingertips of one hand, and press it well into the bottom of the pie plate with the fingertips of the other hand, pressing lightly to seal any cracks.

Dough is easy to lift when wrapped around rolling pin

High dough edge is easy to scallop

3 Using a table knife, trim the pastry even with the outer edge of the plate. Pinch the dough to make the edge stand up. With one forefinger under the dough edge, pinch the top of the edge between your other forefinger and thumb to make a wide scallop.

Thumb and forefingers shape scallops easily

4 Prick the bottom of the pastry shell with a fork to prevent air bubbles from forming during baking. Chill the pastry shell until firm, about 15 minutes. Heat the oven to 400°F. Put the baking sheet in the oven to heat.

5 Line the shell with a double thickness of foil, pressing it well into the bottom edge. Half-fill the foil with dried beans to weigh down the dough. Bake on the baking sheet until the edge is set, 12–15 minutes.

6 Remove the foil and beans. Reduce the oven temperature to 350°F, and continue baking until the bottom of the pastry shell is firm, 5–10 minutes longer. Transfer the pastry shell to the wire rack to cool.

3 MAKE THE FILLING AND FINISH THE PIE

Strawberries are easy to hull with point of small sharp knife

Moist green hulls indicate freshness

1 Hull the strawberries, using the tip of the small knife. Wash them only if they are dirty. Set aside 8 of the strawberries for decoration.

2 In the food processor, work the strawberries to a coarse purée. Alternatively, chop the strawberries with the chef's knife.

3 Pour the cream into a chilled bowl, and whip with the electric mixer or a hand whisk until soft peaks form and the cream just holds its shape; cover and chill the cream.

Cream thickens faster when whipped in chilled bowl

Soft peaks form when beaters are lifted

4 Sprinkle the gelatin evenly over the water in a small saucepan. Let soak, about 5 minutes. The gelatin will soften to a spongy consistency.

5 In a medium heavy-based saucepan, combine the puréed strawberries, sugar, and egg yolks.

6 Heat the mixture, whisking constantly, just until it comes to a boil, 2–3 minutes; it will lighten and thicken slightly. Pour the mixture into a medium bowl. Let cool to tepid.

Whisk ingredients together thoroughly before mixture boils

7 Set the softened gelatin over low heat, and melt it until pourable, shaking the saucepan occasionally, 1–2 minutes; do not stir the gelatin, or it may cook into strings.

8 Beat the tepid strawberry and egg yolk mixture with the electric mixer until light and frothy, 1–2 minutes. Pour the melted gelatin into the mixture, and whisk until cool.

9 Set the bowl of strawberry filling in a larger bowl half-filled with ice water, and stir gently until the mixture starts to thicken, 2–3 minutes. Remove the bowl from the bowl of ice water.

Mixture will start to set as soon as it is cold

Stir mixture gently but constantly with rubber spatula so it thickens evenly

10 Add the chilled whipped cream, and fold together gently, scooping under the mousse and turning the mixture over. At the same time, turn the bowl counter-clockwise.

11 Pour the strawberry filling into the prepared pastry shell, and chill until set, 1–2 hours. Just before serving, slice the reserved strawberries just to the stem ends so they remain intact. Gently press each strawberry flat into a fan with your thumb.

TO SERVE

Arrange the fans on the set pie filling, and place a mint sprig at each hull end. Transfer the pie plate to a serving platter. Cut the pie into wedges, using a knife dipped in hot water.

Dark chocolate crust forms frame around pale pink filling

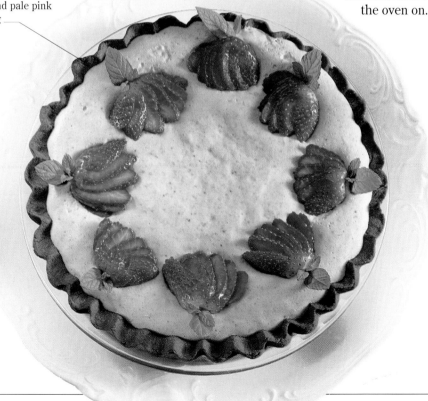

COCONUT MOUSSE PIE

Fresh strawberries are replaced by a filling flavored with toasted coconut and coconut milk. Canned coconut milk is available in most Asian food stores.

1 Omit the strawberries. Make and chill the pastry dough, and line the pie plate as directed. Trim the edge of the dough even with the outer edge of the plate. With the tines of a table fork, mark lines around the edge of the pastry shell. Blind bake the pastry shell as directed. Leave the oven on.

2 Spread 1 cup unsweetened shredded coconut on a baking tray, and toast in the heated oven until golden brown, about 5 minutes. Stir occasionally so it browns evenly.

3 Whip the cream as directed.

4 Prepare the gelatin and make the filling as directed, adding 1 cup canned coconut milk to the egg yolks in place of the strawberry purée. Bring the mixture just to a boil, then let cool. If the mixture separates, whisk it to mix; then stir in half of the toasted coconut. Add the melted gelatin, and fold in the whipped cream as directed.

5 Fill the pie as directed. Chill until the filling is set, 1–2 hours.

6 Coarsely grate 2 oz semisweet chocolate. Sprinkle alternate bands of grated chocolate and the remaining toasted coconut crosswise over the pie, and cut it into wedges for serving.

AMELIA SIMMONS' MOLASSES PUMPKIN PIE

🍽 SERVES 6 🥄 WORK TIME 45–50 MINUTES* 🍲 BAKING TIME 45–50 MINUTES**

EQUIPMENT

chef's knife

small knife

pastry brush

9-inch pie plate

metal spatula

food processor

bowls

rolling pin

slotted spoon

colander

large pot with lid

wire rack

aluminum foil

electric mixer

baking sheet

strainer

scissors

dried beans

rubber spatula

metal skewer

The first American cookbook, written by Amelia Simmons in 1796, included a pumpkin pie similar to this one. She suggested sweetening the filling with economical blackstrap molasses, but I've added a generous amount of sugar because it is more to our modern taste.

GETTING AHEAD

The dough can be made and the pumpkin can be cooked up to 2 days ahead. Keep them both, tightly wrapped, in the refrigerator. The pie is best eaten on the day of baking.

plus 45 minutes chilling
**plus 15 minutes blind baking*

SHOPPING LIST

2½–3 lb	piece of pumpkin
2	eggs
¾ cup	heavy cream
¼ cup	sugar
½ tsp	ground ginger
½ tsp	ground nutmeg
¼ tsp	ground mace
¼ cup	blackstrap molasses
For the shortcrust pastry dough	
1½ cups	flour
¼ tsp	salt
1½ tbsp	sugar (optional)
¼ cup	vegetable shortening
¼ cup	unsalted butter, more for pie plate
3–4 tbsp	cold water, more if needed

INGREDIENTS

pumpkin †

blackstrap molasses

vegetable shortening

sugar

flour

heavy cream

ground nutmeg

eggs

ground ginger

unsalted butter

ground mace

†1½ cups canned pumpkin purée can also be used

ORDER OF WORK

1 MAKE THE SHORTCRUST PASTRY DOUGH; COOK AND PUREE THE PUMPKIN

2 LINE THE PIE PLATE; MAKE THE DECORATION; BLIND BAKE SHELL

3 PREPARE THE FILLING AND BAKE THE PIE

1 MAKE THE SHORTCRUST PASTRY DOUGH; COOK AND PUREE THE PUMPKIN

1 Make the shortcrust pastry dough (see box, page 60). While the dough is chilling, prepare the pumpkin. Scoop out the seeds, and pull out the fibrous threads from the pumpkin; discard them.

ANNE SAYS
"A large metal spoon is the best tool for removing pumpkin seeds."

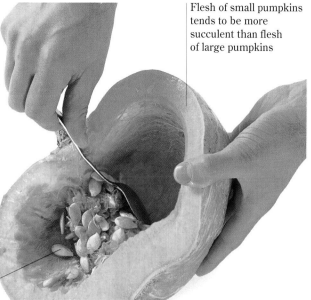

Flesh of small pumpkins tends to be more succulent than flesh of large pumpkins

Seeds detach easily when pumpkin is ripe

2 Cut the pumpkin skin and flesh lengthwise into wedges, then crosswise into large chunks; put into the large pot. Pour in enough water to come one-quarter of the way up the pumpkin, cover, and simmer until the flesh is tender, 25–30 minutes.

When cooked, pumpkin flesh can be easily scraped from skin

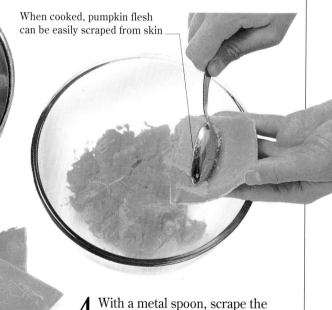

3 With the slotted spoon, transfer the pumpkin to the colander, and discard the cooking water.

4 With a metal spoon, scrape the pumpkin flesh into a bowl, and discard the skin.

5 Transfer the pumpkin flesh to the food processor, and purée until smooth. Alternatively, purée the flesh in batches in a blender.

6 Work the pumpkin purée through the strainer to remove any fibers. There should be about 1 1/2 cups pumpkin purée.

HOW TO MAKE SHORTCRUST PASTRY DOUGH IN A FOOD PROCESSOR

Shortcrust pastry dough can be made in a food processor, fitted with a metal blade. Water is added gradually, with the blades turning. Sugar is an optional ingredient.

1 Put the flour into a food processor. Add the salt, and sugar, if using, and blend, about 5 seconds.

2 Cut the shortening and butter into small pieces, and add the pieces to the flour mixture.

3 Work the mixture, using the pulse button, until it resembles coarse crumbs, 10–15 seconds.

4 Sprinkle the cold water over the mixture, 1 tbsp at a time, and work, using the pulse button, just until the crumbs start sticking together, 10–15 seconds. If the crumbs are dry and do not stick, add 1–2 tbsp more water.

! TAKE CARE !
If too much water is added, the dough will be sticky and the pastry will be tough.

As water is mixed in, crumbs become larger and dough begins to hold together

5 Transfer the dough to the work surface, and press lightly into a ball. Wrap the dough tightly, and chill until firm, about 30 minutes.

LINE THE PIE PLATE; MAKE THE DECORATION; BLIND BAKE SHELL

1 With the pastry brush, brush the pie plate with melted butter. Lightly flour the work surface, and roll out the chilled dough into a round 2 inches larger than the top of the pie plate.

2 Wrap the dough around the rolling pin and drape it over the plate.

Dough hangs over edge of pie plate

3 Gently lift the edge of the dough with one hand, and press it well into the bottom of the plate with the other hand, pressing gently to seal any cracks.

! TAKE CARE !
Be careful not to stretch the dough or it will shrink when baked.

After chilling, dough is pliable and easy to mold

Excess dough will be trimmed and reserved to make maple-leaf decoration

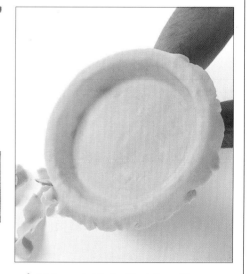

4 Using a table knife, trim off excess dough even with the outer edge of the plate, and chill the trimmings. Pinch the dough edge between thumb and forefinger to make it stand up.

6 With your fingertips, push one point toward the center of the shell, and the next point toward the edge. Continue around the edge. Prick the bottom of the pastry shell with a fork. Chill until firm, about 15 minutes. Heat the oven to 400°F. Put the baking sheet in the oven to heat.

5 Feather the edge of the pastry shell: with the scissors, make ½-inch diagonal incisions at ½-inch intervals around the rim.

Shape "feathers" carefully with fingertips so they do not break

7 Meanwhile, roll out the dough trimmings, and cut out 3 maple-leaf shapes about 3 inches across, using a tracing from an illustration of a maple leaf as a guide, if necessary. Mark veins on the leaves with the back of the small knife; set the leaves on a plate, and chill.

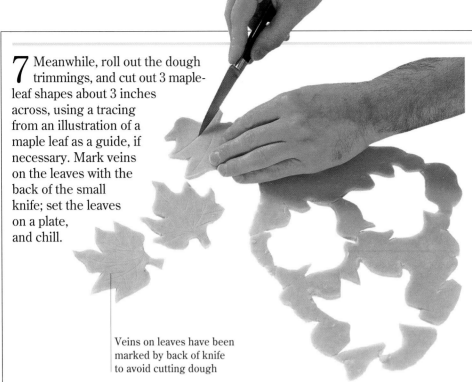

Veins on leaves have been marked by back of knife to avoid cutting dough

8 Line the prepared pastry shell with a double thickness of foil, pressing it well into the bottom edge. Half-fill the foil with dried beans or rice to weigh down the dough.

9 Bake the shell on the baking sheet in the heated oven until set and the shell rim just starts to brown, about 10 minutes. Remove the foil and beans or rice. Reduce the oven temperature to 350° F. Continue baking until lightly browned, about 5 minutes longer.

10 Transfer the blind-baked pastry shell to the wire rack, and let cool slightly.

3 PREPARE THE FILLING AND BAKE THE PIE

2 Beat the mixture with the electric mixer until thoroughly mixed. Alternatively, beat the mixture with a hand whisk.

1 Beat the eggs lightly until mixed. Add the cream and beaten eggs to the pumpkin purée.

Electric mixer makes light work of mixing pumpkin in filling

V A R I A T I O N

PUMPKIN CRUNCH PIE

In this version, a pecan-crunch topping is sprinkled over the filling during baking.

3 Add the sugar, ground ginger, nutmeg, and mace. Pour in the molasses, and beat to combine.

4 Pour the pumpkin mixture into the shell, and bake on the baking sheet in the heated oven, 20 minutes.

5 Add the leaves to the baking sheet, and continue baking the pie with the leaves until the filling is firm, and the metal skewer inserted in the center comes out clean, 25–30 minutes longer. Transfer the pumpkin pie and the maple leaves to the wire rack, and let cool.

1 Omit ground ginger and mace. Cook and purée the pumpkin as directed.
2 Make and chill the dough, and blind bake the pastry shell as directed.
3 Make the filling, adding 1/2 tsp each of ground nutmeg and cinnamon, 1/4 tsp ground allspice, and a pinch of ground cloves.
4 Make the topping: coarsely chop 1/2 cup pecans. Sift 1/4 cup flour into a medium bowl. Stir in 1/2 cup rolled oats. Add 3 tbsp unsalted butter, and cut it into small pieces with a pastry blender, or with 2 round-bladed knives. Rub the mixture with your fingertips until coarse crumbs form. Stir in 1/2 cup brown sugar and the chopped pecans.
5 Pour the filling into the pastry shell, and bake in the heated oven, 15 minutes.
6 Sprinkle the topping evenly over the filling, and continue baking the pie until the filling is firm and the topping is crunchy and brown, 30–40 minutes longer.
7 Cut the pie into wedges, and serve with lightly whipped cream, if you like.

Maple leaves suggest autumn and Thanksgiving

†◎¶ TO SERVE
Set the maple leaves on the filling, then transfer the pie plate to a serving platter. Cut the pie into wedges, and serve from the plate at room temperature, with lightly whipped cream, if you like.

Molasses gives a gleaming dark finish to pumpkin pie

ALMOND AND RASPBERRY TART

Linzertorte

🍽 SERVES 6–8 ⏲ **WORK TIME 30–35 MINUTES*** 🍲 **BAKING TIME 40–45 MINUTES**

EQUIPMENT

9-inch tart pan with removable base

strainers

pastry brush

citrus juicer

pastry scraper

metal spatula

food processor †

grater

bowls

wire rack

medium saucepan

baking sheet

fluted pastry wheel

rolling pin

wooden spoon

parchment paper

† rotary cheese grater can also be used

INGREDIENTS

whole blanched almonds

raspberries

flour

unsalted butter

granulated sugar

egg yolk

lemon

ground cinnamon

confectioners' sugar

ground cloves

Now a Viennese specialty, this tart of buttery almond pastry and raspberry filling probably originated in the town of Linz in Austria. A lattice of pastry and a dusting of confectioners' sugar decorate the tart.

GETTING AHEAD

The tart mellows if it is baked 1–2 days ahead and stored in an airtight container. Sprinkle it with confectioners' sugar about 30 minutes before serving.

*plus 1 ¹/₄–2 ¹/₄ hours chilling time

SHOPPING LIST

1¹/₄ pints	raspberries
6–8 tbsp	granulated sugar
1–2 tbsp	confectioners' sugar
	For the almond pastry dough
1	lemon
1¹/₂ cups	whole blanched almonds
1 cup	flour, more if needed
¹/₂ tsp	ground cinnamon
1	pinch of ground cloves
¹/₂ cup	unsalted butter, more for tart pan
1	egg yolk
¹/₂ cup	granulated sugar
¹/₄ tsp	salt

ORDER OF WORK

1 MAKE THE ALMOND PASTRY DOUGH; MAKE THE RASPBERRY FILLING

2 LINE THE TART PAN AND FINISH THE TART

1   MAKE THE ALMOND PASTRY DOUGH; MAKE THE RASPBERRY FILLING

1 Grate the zest from the lemon onto a piece of parchment paper. Halve the lemon and squeeze the juice from 1 half; you should have about 1½ tbsp.

2 Put the whole almonds in the food processor, add half of the flour to protect the almonds from becoming oily, and finely grind. Alternatively, grind the almonds by themselves in a rotary cheese grater.

3 Sift the remaining flour onto the work surface, with the cinnamon and cloves. Mix in the nuts, then make a well. Pound the butter to soften it. Put the butter, egg yolk, sugar, salt, lemon juice, and zest into the well.

4 Using your fingertips, work the ingredients in the well until thoroughly mixed. Draw in the flour, and work it into the other ingredients until coarse crumbs form.

5 Press the dough into a ball, adding a little more flour if it is sticky. Lightly flour the work surface.

Break up raspberries with spoon

6 Blend the dough by pushing it away from you with the heel of your hand. Then gather it up with the pastry scraper, and continue to blend until it is very smooth and peels away from the work surface in one piece, 1–2 minutes. Shape into a ball, wrap tightly, and chill until firm, 1–2 hours. While it is chilling, make the filling.

7 Pick over the raspberries; wash them only if dirty. Put the sugar and raspberries in the saucepan. Cook, stirring, until they form a thick pulpy jam, 10–12 minutes. Set aside to cool.

8 With the back of the wooden spoon, press half of the fruit pulp through a strainer, set over a bowl, to remove the seeds. Stir in the remaining pulp, leaving in seeds for texture.

2 LINE THE TART PAN AND FINISH THE TART

1 Brush the tart pan with melted butter. Lightly flour the work surface; roll out two-thirds of the dough into an 11-inch round. Rewrap and chill the remaining dough.

2 Wrap the dough around the rolling pin, then drape it over the pan. Gently lift the edge of the dough with one hand, and press it into the bottom of the pan with the other hand. Overlap the dough slightly inside the pan rim.

3 Roll the rolling pin over the top of the pan, to cut off the excess dough. Reserve the trimmings. With your thumbs, press the dough evenly up the side of the tart pan to increase the height of the shell.

4 Spread the filling over the bottom of the shell. Roll out the remaining dough; trim to a 6- x 12-inch rectangle. Reserve the trimmings. Cut the dough into twelve $\frac{1}{2}$-inch strips with the pastry wheel.

Fluted pastry wheel is simple to use

5 Carefully arrange half of the strips from left to right across the tart, about $\frac{3}{4}$-inch apart. Turn the tart 45° and arrange the remaining strips diagonally over the first strips to form a lattice. Flour the rolling pin and roll it over the edge of the pan to trim the overhanging dough strips.

Metal spatula makes it easy to lift fragile strips of dough

Space strips as evenly as possible

6 Roll all the dough trimmings into a long cylinder, then roll out thinly. Using the fluted pastry wheel, cut 3–4 $\frac{1}{2}$-inch strips to go around the edge of the tart. Brush the edge of the tart with cold water. Arrange the strips around the edge, pressing with your fingertips. Chill until the dough is firm, about 15 minutes.

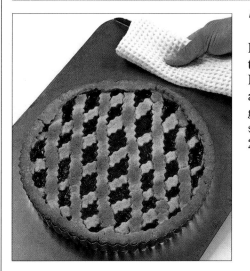

7 Heat the oven to 375° F. Put the baking sheet in the oven to heat. Bake the tart on the baking sheet until the pastry begins to brown, 15 minutes. Reduce the oven temperature to 350° F, and continue baking until the tart is golden brown and just beginning to shrink from the side of the tart pan, 25–30 minutes longer.

8 Transfer the tart to the wire rack, and let cool slightly. Set the tart pan on a bowl to loosen and remove the side. Slide the tart from the pan base onto the wire rack, and let cool completely.

Bowl gives firm support to tart pan

🍽 TO SERVE
About 30 minutes before serving, dust the entire surface of the tart with the confectioners' sugar. Serve the tart cut into wedges.

Moist filling dissolves sugar and shows through the lattice

HAZELNUT AND APRICOT TART

Curved strips of hazelnut pastry top an apricot filling baked in a hazelnut pastry shell.

1 Omit the raspberries. Substitute hazelnuts for the almonds. Spread on a baking sheet, and toast in a 350° F oven until lightly browned, 10–12 minutes. Rub in a dish towel to remove the skins, then let cool. Make the pastry dough, and line the tart pan as directed.

2 Coarsely chop 1½ cups pitted dried apricots. In a saucepan, combine the apricots, 2–3 tbsp sugar, and water to cover. Simmer until reduced to a pulpy jam, 8–10 minutes. Let cool.

3 Spread the filling over the bottom of the shell. Roll out two-thirds of the remaining dough into a 2½- x 12-inch strip. With a fluted pastry wheel, cut lengthwise into six ⅜-inch strips. Cut the strips in half. Set the end of 1 strip in the center of the tart, curve it, and attach the other end to the outer edge. Continue, spacing strips evenly around the tart. Trim the ends. Roll out remaining dough, cut strips, and arrange around edge of tart as directed. Roll out the trimmings. Cut 1 round with a 2-inch fluted cookie cutter, and a second with a 1-inch fluted cutter, and set in the center of the tart.

4 Chill, bake, and serve as directed.

BRAIDED THREE-NUT PIE

 SERVES 6–8 WORK TIME 35–40 MINUTES* BAKING TIME 45–50 MINUTES**

EQUIPMENT

chef's knife

whisk

pastry brush

small knife

rice‡

8-inch square cake pan†

bowls

wooden spoon

rolling pin

small saucepan

aluminum foil

dish towel

baking sheet

rubber spatula

chopping board

strainer

metal skewer

wire racks

† 9-inch round pie plate can also be used
‡ dried beans can also be used

INGREDIENTS

hazelnuts   walnut halves

whole blanched almonds   eggs

flour   vanilla extract

unsalted butter   light brown sugar

milk   vegetable shortening

Inspired by the traditional pecan pie, this pie combines walnuts, hazelnuts, and almonds in a light filling, decorated with braids of pastry. Make your own choice of nuts, or select your individual favorite. I like to bake this pie in a square cake pan for an unusual presentation.

GETTING AHEAD

The pie pastry dough can be made up to 2 days ahead and kept, tightly wrapped, in the refrigerator. The pie can be baked up to 1 day ahead and stored in an airtight container.

*plus 45 minutes chilling
**plus 15 minutes blind baking

SHOPPING LIST

½ cup	walnut halves
½ cup	whole blanched almonds
¼ cup	hazelnuts
¼ cup	unsalted butter, more for cake pan
4	eggs
1½ cups	light brown sugar
1 tsp	vanilla extract
¼ tsp	salt
1 tbsp	milk, for glaze
	For the pie pastry dough
2½ cups	flour
½ tsp	salt
¾ cup	vegetable shortening
6–7 tbsp	cold water, more if needed

ORDER OF WORK

1 MAKE THE PIE PASTRY DOUGH, LINE THE PAN, AND BLIND BAKE THE SHELL

2 PREPARE THE FILLING AND FILL THE PASTRY SHELL

3 FINISH AND BAKE THE PIE

1 MAKE THE PIE PASTRY DOUGH, LINE THE PAN, AND BLIND BAKE THE SHELL

1 Make the pie pastry dough (see box, below). Brush the cake pan with melted butter. Lightly flour the work surface. Roll out two-thirds of the dough, and trim it to a 10-inch square. Return the remaining dough to the refrigerator.

2 Wrap the dough around the rolling pin and drape it over the cake pan.

Use rolling pin to lift dough so it does not tear

HOW TO MAKE PIE PASTRY DOUGH

Pie pastry dough is the easiest and most versatile of all doughs and is made with all shortening. The ingredients are mixed as quickly as possible in a bowl. The dough can also be made in a food processor, using the method given for Shortcrust Pastry Dough (see box, page 60). For a slightly sweeter pastry, add 1–2 tbsp sugar with the flour.

Tap strainer to speed up sifting

1 Sift the flour and salt into a bowl. Add the shortening to the bowl.

2 Cut the shortening into the flour mixture with 2 round-bladed table knives or a pastry blender.

3 With your fingertips, rub the shortening into the flour until the mixture forms coarse crumbs, lifting and crumbling the mixture to help aerate it.

4 Sprinkle the water over the mixture, 1 tbsp at a time, and mix lightly with a fork.

Handle dough lightly or it will become elastic and hard to roll

5 When the crumbs are moist enough to start sticking together, press the dough lightly into a ball, wrap it tightly, and chill until firm, about 30 minutes.

3 Lift the edge of the dough with the fingertips of one hand, and press well into the bottom edges and up the sides of the pan with the fingertips of the other hand.

ANNE SAYS
"The height of pan sides may vary, but dough need not reach the rim when pressed up the pan sides."

Press dough into bottom edge with fingertips

Seams of dough are pressed neatly into corners

4 Using a round-bladed table knife, trim the dough inside the pan, so that the shell is 1½ inches deep.

5 Prick the bottom of the pastry shell with a fork to prevent air bubbles from forming during cooking. Chill until firm, about 15 minutes. Press the dough trimmings into the remaining dough, and chill. Heat the oven to 400°F. Put the baking sheet in the oven to heat.

6 Line the shell with a double thickness of foil, pressing it well into the corners. Half-fill the foil with rice. Bake the shell on the baking sheet in the heated oven until set, about 10 minutes.

7 Remove the foil and rice, and continue baking, about 5 minutes longer.

Once dough is set, lining of foil filled with rice is removed so pastry can dry in oven

8 Let the pastry shell cool slightly in the pan on the wire rack. Reduce the oven temperature to 350°F.

2 PREPARE THE FILLING AND FILL THE PASTRY SHELL

1 Set aside one-third of the walnuts and almonds for decoration. Spread the remainder on the baking sheet and toast in the oven until lightly browned, stirring occasionally, 8–10 minutes. Remove the nuts from the baking sheet.

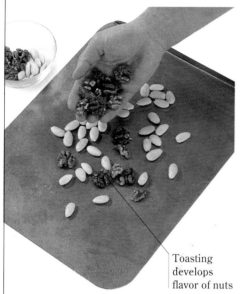

Toasting develops flavor of nuts

2 Toast the hazelnuts as for the walnuts and almonds, allowing 12–15 minutes. Leave the oven on. While the hazelnuts are still hot, rub in a rough dish towel to remove the skins. Let cool.

Leave nuts quite coarse to add texture

3 With the chef's knife, roughly chop the toasted walnuts, almonds, and hazelnuts. In the small saucepan, melt the butter. Let cool.

4 Put the eggs into a medium bowl. Add the brown sugar, and stir the eggs and sugar together with the whisk until they are evenly mixed.

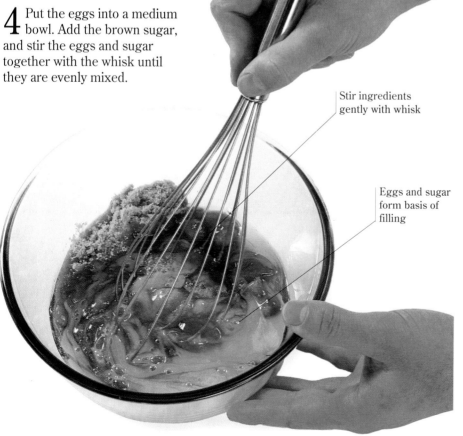

Stir ingredients gently with whisk

Eggs and sugar form basis of filling

5 Add the vanilla extract, salt, and cooled melted butter to the egg mixture, and stir until well combined.

6 Add the toasted chopped walnuts, almonds, and hazelnuts to the filling mixture.

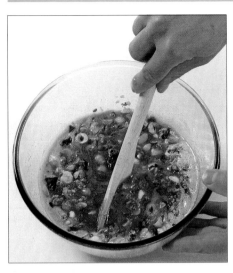

7 With the wooden spoon, stir the nuts into the filling mixture to distribute them evenly.

Rubber spatula helps filling flow

8 Carefully pour the filling into the pastry shell. Set the filled shell aside while making the pastry braids.

3 FINISH AND BAKE THE PIE

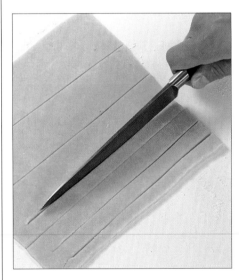

1 Lightly flour the work surface. Roll out the remaining dough, and trim it to an 8-inch square. Cut it into 4 even pieces. Leaving the dough attached at the top, cut each piece into 3 strips.

Braid strips carefully so they do not stretch or tear

2 Braid 3 strips together, lifting them carefully over each other, so they lie flat. Pinch the ends together, trim evenly, and put the braid on a plate. Repeat with the remaining strips to make 4 braids. Chill.

3 Meanwhile, bake the pie on the baking sheet in the heated oven just until it starts to set, 8–10 minutes. Lay the braids along the edges of the filling, and brush them with the milk to glaze. Arrange the reserved nuts decoratively on top of the filling.

ANNE SAYS
"Chilling the braids helps them keep their shape while baking."

4 Continue baking until the metal skewer inserted in the center of the pie comes out clean, 35–40 minutes longer.

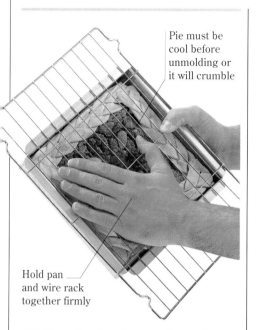

Pie must be cool before unmolding or it will crumble

Hold pan and wire rack together firmly

5 Transfer the pie to a wire rack. Let cool to room temperature. When cool, transfer the wire rack to the top of the pan, turn both over together, then carefully lift off the pan. Set a second rack on the pie base, and turn both over so the pie is right-side up. Slide the pie onto a serving platter.

⦿ TO SERVE
Serve the pie at room temperature. Cut into squares, and transfer to individual plates.

Pastry braids make festive finish

VARIATION
CLASSIC PECAN PIE

In this holiday favorite, walnuts, almonds, and hazelnuts are omitted, and only pecans are used. The sweet nut filling invites a simple accompaniment of fresh heavy cream. The edge of the pastry shell is scalloped with a dessert spoon – a simple method that creates a striking effect.

1 Omit the walnuts, whole blanched almonds, and hazelnuts.
2 Make the pie pastry dough as directed in the box on page 69, using 1½ cups flour, ¼ tsp salt, ½ cup vegetable shortening, and 3–4 tbsp cold water, more if needed.
3 Chill the dough as directed, about 30 minutes.

4 Brush a 9-inch pie plate with melted butter. Roll out the dough into a round 2 inches larger than the top of the pie plate. Wrap the dough around the rolling pin, then drape it over the plate. Gently lift the edge of the dough, then press it well into the bottom edge of the pie plate. Using a round-bladed table knife, trim the excess dough even with the outer edge of the plate.

5 Spoon-scallop the edge: press the rounded tip of a spoon around the edge of the shell at close intervals. Chill; blind bake the shell as directed.
6 Coarsely chop ½ cup pecans. Do not toast them. Make the filling as directed, replacing the mixed nuts with the pecans. Pour the filling into the pastry shell. Arrange 1 cup pecan halves on top. Bake on the baking sheet in the 350°F oven, 40–45 minutes. Serve from the pie plate, at room temperature, cut into wedges.

Whole nuts decorate the serving platter

CARAMELIZED UPSIDE-DOWN MANGO TARTLETS

Tartelettes Tatin aux Mangues

🍽 SERVES 6 🥣 WORK TIME 40–45 MINUTES* 🍲 BAKING TIME 20–25 MINUTES

EQUIPMENT

 chef's knife

 metal spatula

small knife

 food processor †

 six 4-inch baking dishes ‡

bowls

dish towel

 heavy-based saucepan

baking sheet

 rolling pin

 rubber spatula

chopping board

† blender can also be used

‡ six 4-inch tartlet pans with solid bases can also be used

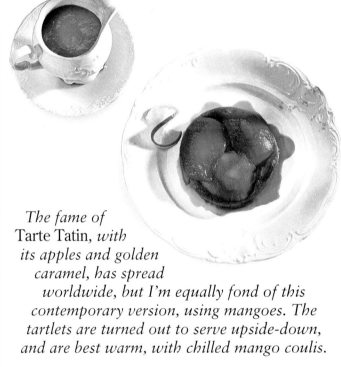

The fame of Tarte Tatin, with its apples and golden caramel, has spread worldwide, but I'm equally fond of this contemporary version, using mangoes. The tartlets are turned out to serve upside-down, and are best warm, with chilled mango coulis.

GETTING AHEAD

The dough can be made up to 2 days ahead and kept, tightly wrapped, in the refrigerator. The tartlets can be baked, and the coulis made up to 8 hours ahead. Refrigerate the coulis, and leave the tartlets in the dishes. To serve, warm the tartlets in a 350°F oven, about 10 minutes, then turn out.

*plus 45 minutes chilling time

SHOPPING LIST

1 cup	sugar
1/2 cup	water
4	medium mangoes, total weight about 2 1/2 lb.
	juice of 1/2 lime
1–2 tbsp	confectioners' sugar (optional)
	For the pâte sucrée dough
6 tbsp	unsalted butter
3	egg yolks
1/2 tsp	vanilla extract
1 1/2 cups	flour, more if needed
1/3 cup	sugar
1/4 tsp	salt

INGREDIENTS

mangoes · unsalted butter · vanilla extract

lime juice · sugar

flour · egg yolks

ANNE SAYS
"Use mangoes that are ripe but still firm, so they do not produce too much juice during cooking."

ORDER OF WORK

1 MAKE THE DOUGH AND CARAMEL SYRUP

2 PREPARE THE MANGOES; FILL AND BAKE THE TARTLETS

3 MAKE THE MANGO COULIS; UNMOLD THE TARTLETS

1 MAKE THE DOUGH AND CARAMEL SYRUP

1 Make and chill the pâte sucrée dough (see box, page 76). Make the caramel syrup: put the sugar and water in the saucepan, and heat gently until dissolved, stirring occasionally. Boil, without stirring, until the mixture starts to turn golden around the edge.

Bubbles start to break more slowly and syrup turns golden

Boil sugar syrup briskly so water evaporates rapidly

! TAKE CARE !
Do not stir the sugar syrup during boiling or it may crystallize.

2 Lower the heat, and continue cooking, swirling the saucepan once or twice so the syrup colors evenly, until the caramel is golden.

! TAKE CARE !
Cook the caramel only until medium gold; if too dark it will become bitter when it cooks further in the oven.

3 Remove the saucepan from the heat, and immediately plunge the base of the saucepan into a bowl of cold water until cooking stops.

4 Pour about one-sixth of the caramel into the bottom of a baking dish. Working quickly, tilt the dish so the bottom is coated with a thin, even layer. Repeat with the remaining dishes. Let cool.

Tip and rotate dish to spread caramel evenly

2 PREPARE THE MANGOES; FILL AND BAKE THE TARTLETS

2 Cut each mango lengthwise on both sides of the pit so the knife just misses the pit. Cut the remaining mango flesh away from each pit in 2 long slices, and set aside for the coulis. Discard the pits.

Trim as close to pit as possible

1 Peel each mango with the small knife, taking care to remove the minimum amount of mango flesh with the peel.

3 Cut each of the large pieces of mango into 3 diagonal slices. Arrange 3 slices, cut-side up, on top of the caramel in 1 dish. Repeat until all the dishes are filled. Add the remaining slices to the mango for the coulis.

4 Lightly flour the work surface. With your hands, shape the dough into a cylinder about 12 inches long. Cut the cylinder into 6 equal pieces. Shape each piece into a ball.

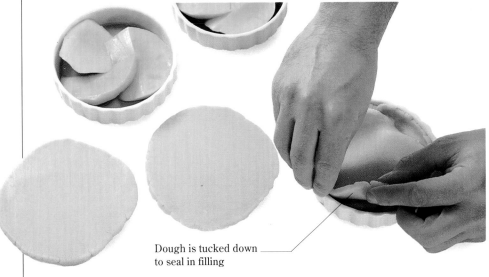

Dough is tucked down to seal in filling

5 Roll out each ball into a 5-inch round. Drape one of the rounds over a baking dish, and tuck the edge down around the mango slices. Repeat for the remaining tartlets. Chill until the dough is firm, about 15 minutes. Heat the oven to 400°F. Bake the tartlets on the baking sheet in the heated oven, 20–25 minutes.

Dough lid will become tartlet base

HOW TO MAKE PATE SUCREE DOUGH IN A FOOD PROCESSOR

Dough should form moist crumbs

1 Cut the butter into pieces. In a small bowl, mix the egg yolks with the vanilla extract. Put the flour in the food processor with the sugar and salt, and blend, about 5 seconds. Add the butter and work the mixture, using the pulse button, until the mixture resembles coarse crumbs, 10–15 seconds.

2 Add the egg yolk and vanilla extract mixture, and continue working the mixture until it resembles small peas, 25–30 seconds. If dough is dry, work in 1–2 tbsp water.

3 Transfer to a lightly floured work surface. Press into a ball, and work with the heel of your hand until smooth. Chill until firm, about 30 minutes.

3 MAKE THE MANGO COULIS; UNMOLD THE TARTLETS

1 Make the mango coulis: put the reserved mango flesh into the food processor or a blender, and purée it.

2 Transfer the purée to a bowl; add the lime juice, and stir it in. Taste the coulis, and add confectioners' sugar, if necessary. Chill.

3 Remove the tartlets from the oven when the crusts are golden brown. Let cool in the dishes, 2–3 minutes. To unmold, set a small plate on top of a baking dish; holding them firmly together, invert them. If any mango slices stick to the dish, remove with a metal spatula and replace on the tartlet. Repeat for the remaining tartlets.

Use dish towel to handle hot baking dish

🍴 TO SERVE
Serve the tartlets at once. Accompany each tartlet with a lime twist, if you like. Pass the mango coulis separately.

Caramel and mango are a perfect combination

V A R I A T I O N

CARAMELIZED UPSIDE-DOWN PEACH TART

Choose firm peaches so the fruit holds its shape during baking.

1 Omit the mangoes and coulis. Make and chill the dough as directed.
2 Make the caramel as directed, and pour it into the base of a 10-inch round baking dish. Let cool.
3 Immerse 2 lb peaches in boiling water, 10 seconds; transfer to a bowl of cold water. Cut 1 peach in half, using the indentation on one side as a guide. Twist with both hands to loosen the halves; then pull them apart. If the flesh clings, loosen it with a knife. Scoop out the pit and discard. Peel off the skin; cut peach halves lengthwise into two. Repeat for remaining peaches.
4 Tightly pack the peach wedges on top of the caramel, rounded side down, in concentric circles.
5 On a lightly floured work surface, roll out the dough into an 11-inch round. Wrap it around the rolling pin, and drape over the dish. Tuck the edge of the dough down around the peaches. Bake the tart as directed, allowing 30–35 minutes. Let the tart cool to tepid.
6 To unmold, set a platter on top of the baking dish. Hold dish and platter firmly together, and invert them; remove the baking dish. Serve at once, cut into wedges.

TRIPLE-DECKER DRIED PEACH TART

Croustade Gasconne aux Pêches

🍴 SERVES 6–8 🥄 WORK TIME 35–40 MINUTES* 🍲 BAKING TIME 55–60 MINUTES

EQUIPMENT

10-inch springform pan

chef's knife

small knife

pastry brush

bowls

wire rack

saucepans

pastry scraper

strainers

baking sheet

petal-shaped cookie cutter

rolling pin

metal skewer

aluminum foil

chopping board

In the Gascony region of southwestern France, dried fruit is popular, eaten simply as a candy. In this ideal winter dessert, dried peaches flavored with peach liqueur are layered in a pastry case, which, in French, is called a croustade. Lemon sorbet would be a delicious accompaniment.

GETTING AHEAD

The dough can be prepared up to 2 days ahead and kept, tightly wrapped, in the refrigerator. The filling can be made up to 2 days ahead and kept in the refrigerator. Assemble and bake the tart not more than 8 hours before serving.

plus 1 hour chilling and 2–3 hours soaking

SHOPPING LIST

2 cups	dried peaches
1 cup + 2 tbsp	sugar
	juice of ½ lemon
2 tbsp	peach liqueur
2 tbsp	unsalted butter
	For the pâte brisée dough
3 cups	flour, more if needed
¾ cup	unsalted butter, more for springform pan
1½ tsp	salt
1	egg
2	egg yolks
1–2 tbsp	water (optional)

INGREDIENTS

dried peaches

sugar

flour

peach liqueur†

egg yolks

lemon juice

egg

unsalted butter

† Cognac can also be used

ORDER OF WORK

1 SOAK THE PEACHES AND MAKE THE PATE BRISEE DOUGH

2 COOK PEACHES; LINE THE PAN; ASSEMBLE TART

1 SOAK THE PEACHES AND MAKE THE PATE BRISEE DOUGH

Dried peaches are quite leathery before soaking —

1 Put the dried peaches on the chopping board. With the chef's knife, cut the dried peaches crosswise into pieces. Put the pieces into a medium bowl.

2 Pour enough boiling water over the peaches to cover them completely. Leave them to soak, 2–3 hours. While the peaches are soaking, make the pâte brisée dough.

3 Sift the flour onto the work surface. With your fingers, make a well in the center of the flour.

4 Pound the butter with the rolling pin to soften it. Put the butter, salt, egg, and egg yolks into the well. With your fingertips, work the moist ingredients until thoroughly mixed.

Pinch butter with your fingertips to blend —

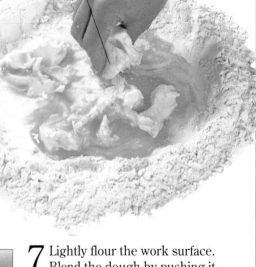

7 Lightly flour the work surface. Blend the dough by pushing it away from you with the heel of your hand, then gathering it up, until it is very smooth and peels away from the work surface in one piece, 1–2 minutes. Shape into a ball, wrap, and chill, about 30 minutes.

5 Draw in the flour with the pastry scraper, and work the flour into the other ingredients with your fingertips until coarse crumbs form.

6 If the dough crumbs are very dry, add 1–2 tbsp cold water. Press the dough into a ball. If it is sticky, work in a little more flour.

2 COOK PEACHES; LINE THE PAN; ASSEMBLE TART

Drain, and discard any cooking liquid

1 Strain the peaches in a strainer, reserving the soaking liquid to help make up the cooking liquid for the peaches. Coarsely chop the peaches.

2 Put the 1 cup sugar into a medium saucepan. Add the peach soaking liquid, then heat until the sugar is dissolved. Add the peaches, and enough water to cover. Bring slowly to a boil and simmer, stirring occasionally, until tender, 20–25 minutes.

3 Drain the peaches thoroughly. In a bowl, combine the peaches with the lemon juice and the peach liqueur. Brush the pan with melted butter.

4 Lightly flour the work surface, and roll out one-third of the dough into a 15-inch round. Wrap the dough around the rolling pin, and drape it over the pan. Lift the edge of the dough with one hand, and let the dough fall into the bottom of the pan. Press it firmly against the bottom and side of the pan with the other hand. Spread one-third of the peaches over the bottom of the shell in an even layer.

Lift dough so it falls gently into pan

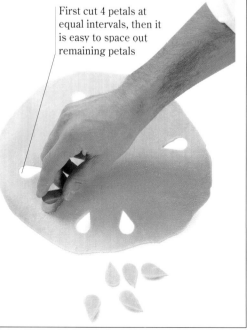

5 Divide the remaining dough into 3 portions. Roll out 1 portion, and trim it to a 10-inch round, then set the round on top of the peaches.

7 Roll out the third portion of dough, and trim it to a 10-inch round. With the cookie cutter, cut out petal shapes close to the edge of the round. Brush the petals with a little cold water, and press them gently onto the center of the round in a circle.

First cut 4 petals at equal intervals, then it is easy to space out remaining petals

6 Spread one-half of the remaining peaches over the dough round. Roll out a second portion of dough, trim it to a 10-inch round, and set the round on top of the peaches. Spread the remaining peaches over the dough round. Brush the dough on the side of the pan with cold water.

8 Carefully lift the dough round onto the final layer of peaches, and press to seal it to the dough on the side of the pan. Trim the excess dough with the small knife and discard. Chill the tart, 30 minutes. Heat the oven to 375° F. Put the baking sheet in the oven to heat.

Remove trimmed dough to leave a neat border

Petal cutouts are evenly spaced

9 Sprinkle the 2 tbsp sugar over the tart. Cut up the butter and dot over the top. Bake on the baking sheet in the heated oven until the metal skewer inserted in the center for 30 seconds is hot to the touch when withdrawn, 55–60 minutes. If the tart browns too quickly, cover it loosely with foil, and reduce the oven temperature to 350° F.

10 Transfer the peach tart to the wire rack, and let cool slightly. Remove the side of the pan, and let the tart cool completely.

🍴 TO SERVE
Slide the tart from the pan base onto a serving platter, cut it into wedges, and serve at room temperature.

Sugar bakes to a rustic topping

Petal cutouts reveal tangy peach filling

VARIATION
TRIPLE-DECKER PRUNE TART

Prunes take the place of dried peaches in this delicious tart – they are soaked in Armagnac, the mellow Gascon version of Cognac.

1 Omit the dried peaches, lemon juice, and peach liqueur.
2 Make and chill the pâte brisée dough as directed.
3 Cut 2 cups moist pitted prunes in half and put them in a medium bowl. If the prunes are dry, first soak them in hot water, 15 minutes, then drain. Add 2 tbsp Armagnac and 1 tbsp sugar to the prunes, and mix.
4 Line the pan and layer the tart as directed, until you come to the third dough round. Stamp out 3 flower shapes from the round at equal intervals with a cookie cutter, and reserve. Set the dough round on top of the final layer of prunes. Trim as directed, and reserve the trimmings.
5 Brush the tips of the flowers with a little cold water, and lay them over the holes at different angles so that the prune filling is visible. Roll out the trimmings, and stamp out 3 more flower shapes. Brush the bases of the flowers with cold water, and press them onto the pastry round in between the flower cutouts. Bake the tart as directed.
6 Serve the tart cut into wedges, accompanied by custard sauce, or vanilla ice cream, if you like.

FRESH MINCEMEAT TART

 SERVES 8   WORK TIME 40–45 MINUTES* BAKING TIME 40–45 MINUTES

EQUIPMENT

10-inch tart pan with removable base   grater

chef's knife

citrus juicer

small knife

vegetable peeler   parchment paper

bowls   chopping board

melon baller

pastry brush   pastry blender †

pastry scraper

wire rack

metal skewer

rolling pin

baking sheet

† 2 round-bladed table knives can also be used

INGREDIENTS

flour   lemon

unsalted butter   apple

granulated sugar

light brown sugar

egg   whiskey

chopped candied orange peel

vegetable shortening   slivered almonds

seedless grapes

dark raisins   golden raisins

ground allspice

ground nutmeg   ground cinnamon

Mincemeat, originally a mixture of dried fruit, suet, spices, and a generous dash of alcohol, was developed to preserve meat. Here, fresh fruit is added to the traditional dried fruit and nut mixture to make a delicious filling for this tart.

plus 1 hour chilling time

SHOPPING LIST

1	medium tart apple
1	lemon
1 cup	seedless grapes
1 tbsp	chopped candied orange peel
3 tbsp	slivered almonds
1/4 tsp	each ground cinnamon, nutmeg, and allspice
1/2 cup	each dark raisins and golden raisins
1/2 cup	light brown sugar
3 tbsp	whiskey
	whiskey hard sauce (see box, page 84) to serve (optional)
	For the shortcrust pastry dough
2 1/2 cups	flour
1 1/2 tbsp	granulated sugar
1/2 tsp	salt
6 tbsp	vegetable shortening
6 tbsp	unsalted butter, more for tart pan
6–7 tbsp	cold water, more if needed
1	egg plus 1/2 tsp salt for glaze

ORDER OF WORK

1 MAKE THE SHORTCRUST PASTRY DOUGH; LINE THE PAN

2 MAKE THE FILLING AND LATTICE; BAKE THE TART

1 MAKE THE SHORTCRUST PASTRY DOUGH; LINE THE PAN

1 Make and chill the pastry dough (see box, page 12). Brush the pan with melted butter. Lightly flour the work surface, and roll out two-thirds of the dough into a 12-inch round. Return the remaining dough to the refrigerator. Wrap the dough around the pin, and drape it over the pan.

If draped gently, dough is not cut by sharp pan edge

2 Gently lift the edge of the dough with one hand, and press it well into the bottom of the pan with the other hand, pressing to seal any cracks. Overlap the dough slightly inside the rim of the pan.

3 Roll the rolling pin over the top of the pan, pressing down to cut off the excess dough. Press the dough trimmings into the remaining dough.

4 With your thumbs, press the dough evenly up the pan side to increase the height of the shell. Chill the shell until firm, about 15 minutes. Meanwhile, make the filling.

2 MAKE THE FILLING AND LATTICE; BAKE THE TART

Lemon juice adds piquancy to filling

2 Grate the zest from the lemon onto a sheet of parchment paper. Halve the lemon, and squeeze the juice. With the small knife, cut the grapes lengthwise in half.

1 Peel the apple, and cut out the flower and stem ends. Halve the apple, then scoop out the core. Set each apple half cut-side down, and cut horizontally into ³/₈-inch slices. Cut the slices lengthwise into ³/₈-inch strips. Gather the strips together and cut crosswise into cubes.

Whiskey accents flavor of dried and fresh fruit

3 Put the apple, grapes, lemon zest and juice, candied orange peel, almonds, ground cinnamon, nutmeg, and allspice, dark and golden raisins, the sugar, and whiskey into a bowl. Stir to combine.

4 Spoon the fresh mincemeat over the bottom of the pastry shell, and gently press it down with the back of a spoon.

5 Make the egg glaze: lightly beat the egg with the salt. Roll out the remaining dough, and trim it to a 10 1/2-inch square. Using the small knife, cut the dough into 3/4-inch strips. There should be 14 strips.

6 Lay 7 strips crosswise over the filling, about 3/4-inch apart, letting the ends hang over the edge of the pan. Fold back alternate strips halfway. Set an eighth strip across the center of the unfolded strips. Unfold the folded strips to cover the crosswise strip, again leaving ends to hang over the edge of the pan. Fold back alternate strips.

Avoid stretching strips of dough

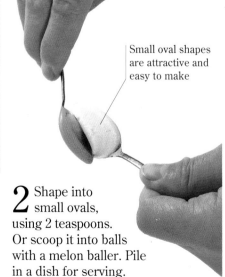

WHISKEY HARD SAUCE

Hard sauce can be made with brandy, rum, or whiskey; it is best known as an accompaniment to English plum pudding.

🍽 SERVES 8

🥄 WORK TIME 15 MINUTES

❄ CHILLING TIME 1–2 HOURS

SHOPPING LIST

1/2 cup	unsalted butter
1/2 cup	sugar
1/4 cup	whiskey

1 Using an electric mixer, beat the butter until creamy. Add the sugar, and continue beating until light and fluffy, 2–3 minutes. Beat in the whiskey, 1 spoonful at a time. Chill the sauce until set, 1–2 hours.

2 Shape into small ovals, using 2 teaspoons. Or scoop it into balls with a melon baller. Pile in a dish for serving.

Small oval shapes are attractive and easy to make

7 Place the ninth strip about ³/₄ inch from the eighth. Continue until half of the surface is latticed. Turn the pan, and repeat the process on the other half of the tart.

8 Brush the ends of the strips with cold water. With your fingertips, seal the strips to the pastry shell, pinching off the overhanging ends. Brush the lattice with the egg glaze.

9 Chill until firm, about 15 minutes. Heat the oven to 350°F. Put the baking sheet in the oven to heat. Bake on the baking sheet until lightly browned, and the metal skewer inserted in the center of the mincemeat for 30 seconds is hot to the touch when withdrawn, 40–45 minutes. Let cool slightly on wire rack; set on a bowl to loosen and remove side.

Side of tart pan falls easily from tart when base is set on bowl

Lattice decoration displays filling of mincemeat

🍴 **TO SERVE**
Slide the tart from the pan base onto a serving platter. Cut the tart into wedges, and serve hot, with hard sauce, if you like.

VARIATION
FESTIVE MINCEMEAT TART
The mincemeat in this holiday tart is made with dried fruit.

1 Omit the apple and grapes. Make and chill the shortcrust pastry dough, and line the tart pan as directed. Grate the lemon zest and squeeze the juice.
2 Chop ¹/₂ cup each dried figs, dried dates, and dried apricots. Combine the chopped fruit, raisins, lemon zest and juice, chopped candied orange peel, almonds, spices, sugar, and whiskey. Spoon the filling over the bottom of the pastry shell, and brush the edge of the shell with cold water. Roll out the remaining dough into an 11-inch round. Fold the dough into quarters.
3 Cut 1-inch diagonal incisions across the folds of the dough. This will make "V" shapes when the dough is unfolded.
4 Unfold the dough, wrap it around the rolling pin, and drape it over the filling. Roll the rolling pin over the pan edge to trim the top crust even with the bottom crust. Press the crusts together to seal, then brush the top of the tart with egg glaze. Chill, bake, unmold, and serve the tart as directed.

— **GETTING AHEAD** —
The mincemeat can be made up to 2 weeks ahead and kept, covered, in the refrigerator. The dough can be made up to 2 days ahead and kept, tightly wrapped, in the refrigerator. Assemble and bake the tart not more than 8 hours ahead.

FLAKY PEAR TARTLETS

EQUIPMENT

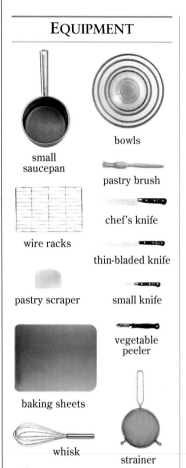

- small saucepan
- bowls
- pastry brush
- chef's knife
- thin-bladed knife
- wire racks
- pastry scraper
- small knife
- vegetable peeler
- baking sheets
- whisk
- strainer
- melon baller †
- wooden spoon
- metal spatula
- chopping board
- rolling pin

† teaspoon or small knife can also be used

INGREDIENTS

- pears
- heavy cream
- flour
- vanilla extract
- unsalted butter
- egg
- granulated sugar
- lemon juice
- confectioners' sugar

These tartlets are a party favorite of mine – a spectacular contrast of hot and cold, they need little last-minute preparation. If you wish, you can save 40–50 minutes work time by substituting 1 lb ready-prepared puff pastry dough for the homemade puff pastry dough used in the recipe.
*plus 1¼ hours chilling time

SHOPPING LIST

4	pears, total weight about 1½ lb
	juice of 1 lemon
¼ cup	granulated sugar
	For the caramel sauce
½ cup	water
¾ cup	granulated sugar
½ cup	heavy cream
	For the puff pastry dough
2 cups	flour
1 cup	unsalted butter, more for baking sheet
1 tsp	salt
1 tsp	lemon juice
½ cup + 2 tbsp	water, more if needed
1	egg plus ½ tsp salt for glaze
	For the Chantilly cream
½ cup	heavy cream
1–2 tsp	confectioners' sugar
½ tsp	vanilla extract

ORDER OF WORK

1 MAKE AND BAKE THE PUFF PASTRY CASES

2 MAKE THE SAUCE AND THE CHANTILLY CREAM

3 PREPARE THE PEAR FANS

4 BROIL THE PEAR FANS AND ASSEMBLE THE TARTLETS

MAKE AND BAKE THE PUFF PASTRY CASES

Cut cleanly through dough from tip to heel of knife blade

1 Make and chill the puff pastry dough (see pages 104–105). Sprinkle 2 baking sheets with cold water. Lightly flour the work surface, then roll out the puff pastry dough, and trim it to an 8-x 20-inch rectangle.

2 Cut the dough in half lengthwise. Cut diagonally at 4-inch intervals along the length of each piece of dough to make a total of 8 diamond shapes.

3 Transfer the pastry dough shapes to the baking sheets, and press them down lightly. Beat the egg with the salt just until mixed, then brush the dough with the glaze.

4 With the tip of the small knife, mark lines parallel to the edges of each one, cutting halfway through the dough to form a lid. Chill until firm, about 15 minutes. Meanwhile, heat the oven to 425°F.

5 Bake the cases in the heated oven until they have started to brown, about 15 minutes. Reduce the oven temperature to 375°F, and continue baking until golden and very crisp, 20–25 minutes longer, reversing level of baking sheets halfway through cooking. Transfer to wire racks to cool.

Cut out lid without slitting through bottom of case

6 With the small knife, cut out the lid from each case. With a teaspoon, carefully scoop out any under-cooked pastry from the base of each pastry case.

2 MAKE THE SAUCE AND THE CHANTILLY CREAM

1 Put the water in the saucepan, add the sugar, and cook over low heat until dissolved, stirring occasionally. Boil, without stirring, until the syrup starts to turn golden. Lower the heat, and continue cooking, swirling the saucepan once or twice so that the syrup colors evenly.

Do not stir during boiling or sugar may crystallize

2 Remove the saucepan from the heat, and let the bubbles subside. Immediately pour in the cream, stirring to mix. Heat gently until the caramel has dissolved. Leave the sauce to cool.

! TAKE CARE !
The caramel will splutter, so stand at arm's length when pouring.

3 Make the Chantilly cream: pour the heavy cream into a chilled bowl, and whip until soft peaks form. Add the confectioners' sugar and vanilla extract, and continue whipping until stiff peaks form. Chill.

3 PREPARE THE PEAR FANS

1 Butter a baking sheet. Peel the pears with the vegetable peeler. Cut out the flower ends with the small knife. Halve the pears, cut out the stem ends, then scoop out the cores with the melon baller, or with a teaspoon or a small knife.

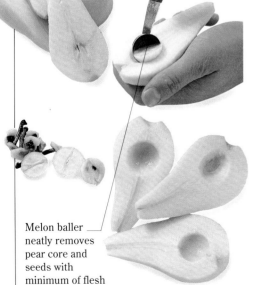

Melon baller neatly removes pear core and seeds with minimum of flesh

2 Set 1 pear half, cut-side down, on the chopping board. Using the thin-bladed knife, cut it lengthwise into thin slices, keeping the slices attached at the stem end. Repeat with the remaining pear halves.

3 With your fingers, flatten the slices of 1 pear half to form a fan. Transfer the pear fan to the prepared baking sheet, using the metal spatula and your fingertips. Repeat with the remaining pear halves.

Buttered baking sheet keeps pears from sticking during cooking

4 Brush each pear fan with the lemon juice. If preparing ahead, cover the pear fans tightly, and chill.

! TAKE CARE !
Be sure that the pear slices are well coated with lemon juice, so they do not discolor on standing.

4 BROIL THE PEAR FANS AND ASSEMBLE THE TARTLETS

1 Heat the broiler. Sprinkle the pear fans with the sugar. Broil about 3–4 inches from the heat until the sugar is caramelized, 3–5 minutes.

2 Transfer the pastry cases to individual plates; spoon a little Chantilly cream into each. Transfer the pear fans to the pastry cases. Drizzle a little cool caramel sauce over each serving, and partially cover each pear fan with a pastry lid.

Spoon Chantilly cream evenly into case

Caramel sauce drizzles easily off spoon

🍽 TO SERVE

Serve at once, while the pear fans are hot and the Chantilly cream is cold. Pass the remaining caramel sauce separately.

Caramel sauce adds sweetness

Crisp puff pastry is a classic container for Chantilly cream topped with broiled pear fan

VARIATION

FLAKY APPLE TARTLETS

Caramelized apple fans replace pear fans in this version of Flaky Pear Tartlets and sit on Chantilly cream in golden puff pastry rounds.

1 Omit the pears. Make and chill the dough as directed. Roll out the dough, and trim it to an 8- x 20-inch rectangle as directed. Cut rounds with a 4-inch fluted cookie cutter, and brush with egg glaze. With a 3-inch fluted cutter or the tip of a small knife, mark a circle on each of the rounds, cutting halfway through the dough. Bake the rounds, and cut out the lids as directed.

2 Make the sauce and Chantilly cream as directed.

3 Peel 4 crisp tart apples (total weight about 1 lb), and prepare and broil in the same way as the pear fans. Put the chilled Chantilly cream and broiled apple fans in the cases as directed. Cover with the lids and serve at once. Pass the sauce separately.

——— GETTING AHEAD ———

The pastry cases can be baked up to 2 days ahead and stored in an airtight container. Make the caramel sauce and Chantilly cream, and prepare the pears not more than 2 hours ahead. Broil the pears and assemble the tartlets just before serving.

FIG AND MULLED WINE TART

🍽 SERVES 6–8　　🥣 WORK TIME 25–30 MINUTES*　　🍲 BAKING TIME 15–20 MINUTES

EQUIPMENT

10-inch
flan ring

whisk

pastry brush

slotted spoon

vegetable
peeler

wire rack

metal spatula

small knife

bowls

pastry
scraper

baking sheet

saucepans, 1 with lid,
1 heavy-based with lid

rolling pin

strainer　　plastic bag

rubber spatula

Fresh figs, with their deep red flesh and delicate flavor, call for the simplest treatment. Here, they are poached briefly in mulled wine syrup.

*plus 1¼ hours chilling time

SHOPPING LIST

1 lb	purple figs
1	orange
1	lemon
1	piece of whole nutmeg
½ cup	sugar
2-inch	piece of cinnamon stick
2	whole cloves
1 tsp	black peppercorns
2 cups	dry red wine
	For the cornmeal pastry dough
1 cup	flour, more if needed
¼ cup	fine yellow cornmeal
⅓ cup	unsalted butter, more for baking sheet and flan ring
1	egg
¼ cup	sugar
¼ tsp	salt
	For the lightened pastry cream
½	vanilla bean
1 cup	milk
3	egg yolks
3 tbsp	sugar
2 tbsp	flour
2 tsp	unsalted butter
6 tbsp	heavy cream

INGREDIENTS

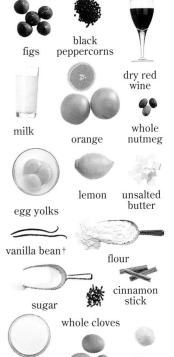

figs

black
peppercorns

dry red
wine

milk

orange

whole
nutmeg

egg yolks

lemon

unsalted
butter

vanilla bean†

flour

sugar

cinnamon
stick

whole cloves

heavy
cream

egg

fine
yellow
cornmeal

†½ tsp vanilla extract can also be used

ORDER OF WORK

1 MAKE THE DOUGH, LINE THE FLAN RING, AND BAKE THE ROUND

2 MAKE THE LIGHTENED PASTRY CREAM

3 MAKE THE SYRUP; POACH THE FIGS; ASSEMBLE TART

1 MAKE THE DOUGH, LINE THE FLAN RING, AND BAKE THE ROUND

1 Sift the flour onto the work surface. Add the cornmeal, and make a well in the center. Pound the butter with the rolling pin to soften it.

2 Beat the egg to mix. Put the butter, egg, sugar, and salt into the well. With your fingertips, work these ingredients until thoroughly mixed.

Use pastry scraper to pull ingredients together

3 Draw in the flour and cornmeal with the pastry scraper, and work them into the other ingredients with your fingers until coarse crumbs form. Press the dough into a ball. If it is sticky, work in a little more flour.

Blend dough with heel of hand

4 Lightly flour the work surface. Blend the dough by pushing it away from you with the heel of your hand, then gathering it up, until it is very smooth and peels away from the surface in one piece, 1–2 minutes. Shape into a ball, wrap it tightly, and chill until firm, about 30 minutes.

5 Set the flan ring on the baking sheet. Brush both with melted butter. Lightly flour the work surface. Roll out dough into an 11-inch round. Wrap it around the rolling pin, then drape it over the ring.

6 Gently lift the edge of the dough with one hand, and press it well into the bottom edge of the flan ring with the other hand, pressing to seal any cracks. Fold over the excess dough inside the flan ring to form a border to the pastry round. Chill until firm, about 15 minutes. Heat the oven to 375°F.

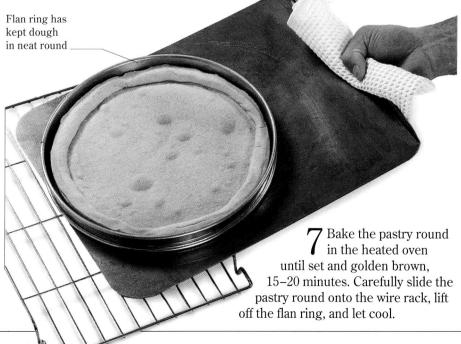

Flan ring has kept dough in neat round

7 Bake the pastry round in the heated oven until set and golden brown, 15–20 minutes. Carefully slide the pastry round onto the wire rack, lift off the flan ring, and let cool.

2 MAKE THE LIGHTENED PASTRY CREAM

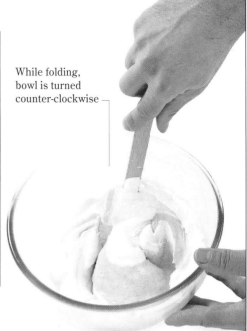

While folding, bowl is turned counter-clockwise

1 Split the vanilla bean, if using. In the heavy-based pan, bring the milk to a boil with the bean. Remove from the heat, cover, and let stand, 10–15 minutes. Whisk the egg yolks and sugar until thick, 2–3 minutes. Stir in flour. Gradually stir in the hot milk until smooth. Pour back into the pan. Bring to a boil over medium heat, whisking constantly until thickened.

! TAKE CARE !
If lumps form, remove from the heat at once, and whisk until smooth again.

2 Lower the heat, and cook, still whisking, until the pastry cream softens slightly, about 2 minutes. Remove from heat, take out vanilla bean, if using, or stir in vanilla extract. Transfer to a bowl, rub the butter over surface of the cream to keep it from forming a skin, and chill, 30 minutes.

ANNE SAYS
"Simmering the pastry cream cooks the flour so it leaves no aftertaste."

3 Pour the heavy cream into a chilled bowl, and whip until soft peaks form; cover, and chill. Add the cream to the chilled pastry cream, and fold together gently but thoroughly, scooping under the pastry cream and turning the mixture over in a rolling motion. Cover, and chill. Meanwhile, make the syrup and poach the figs.

3 MAKE THE SYRUP; POACH THE FIGS; ASSEMBLE TART

Wine will be reduced and enriched

Mixture for poaching figs is aromatic with zest and spices

1 Prick each fig 2 or 3 times with the tines of a fork so that the syrup will penetrate the fruit.

2 Pare the zest from the orange and lemon. Crush the nutmeg in the plastic bag with the rolling pin. Put the zest and nutmeg into a saucepan with the sugar, spices, and peppercorns. Add the wine. Heat, stirring, to dissolve the sugar. Bring just to a boil, then add the figs.

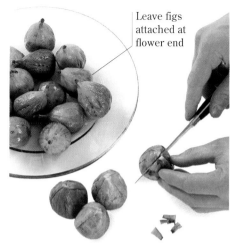

Leave figs attached at flower end

3 Cover, and poach just until the figs are tender, 3–5 minutes. Remove the figs with the slotted spoon, allowing them to drain well, and let cool. Continue simmering the syrup until reduced to ½ cup, 25–30 minutes. Strain the syrup, and let cool.

4 Cut off the stems from the figs; cut the figs into quarters, leaving them attached at the flower end. Slide the pastry round onto a serving plate.

VARIATION

FIG AND MULLED WINE TARTLETS

Sliced figs top individual tartlets in this version of Fig and Mulled Wine Tart.

5 Spread the pastry cream over the pastry round. Arrange the figs in concentric circles on top, and pull each one open slightly. Spoon 1–2 tbsp of the syrup over the figs.

¶◎¶ TO SERVE
Just before serving, spoon the remaining syrup over the tart. Serve at room temperature, cut into wedges.

1 Make and chill the cornmeal pastry dough as directed in the main recipe. Brush a baking sheet with melted butter. Lightly flour the work surface. With your hands, shape the dough into a cylinder about 12 inches long. Cut the cylinder into 6 equal pieces. Shape each piece into a ball, then roll out each ball into a 5-inch round.
2 Set the rounds on the baking sheet, and fold over the edge of each round to form a border. Chill until firm, 15 minutes. Bake the rounds in the oven until golden brown, 12–15 minutes; transfer to a wire rack to cool.
3 Make the pastry cream, and lighten it as directed. Make the mulled wine syrup, and reduce as directed.
4 Transfer the pastry rounds to individual plates, and spread the lightened pastry cream on each one.
5 Do not poach the figs. Cut them lengthwise into thin slices. Overlap in a petal pattern on each tartlet.
6 Brush the fig slices with the syrup; serve any remaining syrup separately.

Mulled wine syrup adds rich color

Poached figs are tender and full of flavor

GETTING AHEAD
The dough can be made up to 2 days ahead and kept, tightly wrapped, in the refrigerator. You can bake the pastry round up to 8 hours ahead; poach the figs, and make the lightened pastry cream up to 2 hours ahead. The tart should not be assembled until just before serving.

MUD PIE

EQUIPMENT

ice cream maker

pastry bag and medium star tube

wooden spoon

whisk

strainers

bowls

food processor†

pastry brush

chef's knife

9-inch pie plate

chopping board

rubber spatula

wire rack

saucepans, 1 heavy-based

baking sheet

†rolling pin and plastic bag can also be used

In this ever-popular, all-American dessert, a chocolate crumb crust is filled with homemade coffee ice cream swirled with chocolate, then piped with cream, and served with hot fudge sauce.

GETTING AHEAD

The pie and fudge sauce can be made up to 3 days ahead. The pie should be kept, tightly wrapped, in the freezer and the fudge sauce kept, covered, in the refrigerator.

*plus 15 minutes chilling and 25–30 minutes baking

SHOPPING LIST

	For the coffee ice cream	
2 ½ cups	milk	
3 tbsp	instant coffee granules	
²/₃ cup	granulated sugar	
8	egg yolks	
2 tbsp	cornstarch	
1 cup	heavy cream	
	For the chocolate crumb crust	
½ cup	unsalted butter, more for pie plate	
½ lb	chocolate wafers	
3 tbsp	granulated sugar	
	For the fudge sauce	
½ cup	whole blanched almonds	
²/₃ cup	heavy cream	
¼ cup	unsalted butter	
½ cup	granulated sugar	
²/₃ cup	light brown sugar	
²/₃ cup	cocoa powder	
	salt	
1 tbsp	dark rum, more to taste	
¾ cup	heavy cream for decoration	

INGREDIENTS

sugar

chocolate wafers

egg yolks

unsalted butter

milk

dark rum

cocoa powder

light brown sugar

whole blanched almonds

heavy cream

instant coffee granules

cornstarch

ANNE SAYS
"You can substitute Oreos for the chocolate wafer cookies."

ORDER OF WORK

1 **PREPARE THE COFFEE CUSTARD; MAKE AND BAKE THE CRUMB CRUST**

2 **TOAST THE ALMONDS; MAKE THE FUDGE SAUCE**

3 **FREEZE THE ICE CREAM AND PIE**

4 **FINISH THE PIE**

1 PREPARE THE COFFEE CUSTARD; MAKE AND BAKE THE CRUMB CRUST

Whisk while pouring

1 Put the milk in a medium heavy-based saucepan with the instant coffee granules, and bring just to a boil, stirring until the coffee granules have dissolved. Set aside one-quarter of the milk mixture. Stir the sugar into the remaining mixture until dissolved.

2 In a medium bowl, whisk the egg yolks with the cornstarch. Add the sweetened hot milk mixture, and whisk just until smooth.

3 Pour the custard back into the saucepan, and cook over medium heat, stirring constantly, just until it comes to a boil and thickens enough to coat the back of a spoon. Your finger will leave a clear trail across the spoon. Custard may curdle if cooked longer.

4 Off the heat, stir in the reserved milk until thoroughly combined. Strain the custard into a cold bowl, and cover tightly to prevent a skin from forming on the surface. Let cool.

Coarse chocolate wafer crumbs will make crisp pie crust

5 Melt the butter. Brush the pie plate with melted butter. Grind the wafers to coarse crumbs in the food processor, using the pulse button. Transfer to a bowl, and add the melted butter and sugar. Stir until all the crumbs are moistened.

Melted butter will bind crumbs and sugar

6 Press the crumbs evenly over the bottom and up the side of the pie plate. Chill until firm, about 15 minutes. Heat the oven to 350°F. Put the baking sheet in the oven to heat.

7 Bake the crumb crust on the baking sheet in the heated oven, 15 minutes. Let cool on the wire rack. The crust will harden as it cools.

2 TOAST THE ALMONDS; MAKE THE FUDGE SAUCE

1 Coarsely chop the almonds. Spread them on the baking sheet; toast in the heated oven until lightly browned, stirring occasionally, 10–12 minutes.

2 In a medium saucepan, heat the heavy cream and butter, stirring occasionally, until the butter melts and the mixture comes just to a boil. Add the sugars and stir them in until dissolved.

Whisk constantly so sauce does not scorch

Cocoa powder gives fudge sauce rich chocolate flavor

3 Sift the cocoa. Whisk it, with a pinch of salt, into the cream and sugar mixture, and bring back to a boil. Gently simmer the fudge sauce, whisking constantly, until the cocoa powder has dissolved, 1–2 minutes longer. Stir in rum.

4 Transfer ½ cup of the fudge sauce to a bowl, and combine with one-half of the almonds. Let cool. Set the remaining sauce and almonds aside.

3 FREEZE THE ICE CREAM AND PIE

1 If the custard has formed a skin, whisk to dissolve it. Pour the coffee custard into the ice cream maker, and freeze until slushy, following the manufacturer's directions. Meanwhile, chill 2 large bowls in the freezer.

2 Pour the cream into one of the chilled bowls, and whisk until soft peaks form. Add the cream to the half-set custard, and continue freezing in the ice cream maker until firm. Freezing time varies with the machine used.

Add whipped cream when ice cream is half set

3 Transfer the coffee ice cream to the second chilled bowl. Add the cooled almond fudge mixture. With 2 round-bladed table knives, cut in the mixture until partly mixed.

ANNE SAYS
"Return the ice cream to the freezer if it starts to melt; otherwise it will seep into the crumb crust."

4 Spread the coffee ice cream and almond fudge mixture over the bottom of the crumb crust. Swirl the top with the back of a metal spoon and freeze, at least 1–2 hours, or up to 3 days.

Use back of spoon to make swirls in ice cream

4 FINISH THE PIE

1 If the pie has been frozen for more than 12 hours, let it soften in the refrigerator, 1 hour. Pour the heavy cream into a chilled bowl, and whip until it forms stiff peaks.

2 Put the cream into the pastry bag fitted with a medium star tube, and pipe rosettes around the edge of the pie. Sprinkle over the reserved almonds. Reheat the fudge sauce.

❗❶❗ TO SERVE
Transfer the pie plate to a serving platter. Serve the pie directly from the plate, cut into wedges. Drizzle hot fudge sauce over the top of each serving, and serve at once.

Almond-studded cream rosettes crown ice cream pie

V A R I A T I O N

GINGERSNAP ICE CREAM PIE

Gingersnap cookies replace the chocolate wafers, and ginger ice cream fills the pie.

1 Omit the instant coffee granules, chocolate wafers, blanched almonds, and rum. Grind or crush ¹/₂ lb gingersnap cookies, then make the crumb crust, line the pie plate, and bake the crumb crust as directed.
2 Finely chop 2 tbsp crystallized ginger. Make the custard as directed, transfer to a bowl, then stir in 1 tsp ground ginger with the chopped ginger. Set the custard aside to cool. Make the fudge sauce as directed, stirring in ¹/₂ tsp vanilla extract in place of the rum. Set aside ¹/₂ cup of the sauce to cool. Set the remaining sauce aside separately.
3 Freeze the ice cream as directed; swirl in the cooled fudge sauce. Spread the ice cream mixture in the shell; freeze as directed.
4 Whip the cream. Pipe swirls and stars of cream around the pie. Reheat the fudge sauce.
5 Serve the pie and fudge sauce as directed.

BAVARIAN PLUM TART

🍽 SERVES 8–10   🥄 WORK TIME 35–40 MINUTES*   🍲 BAKING TIME 50–55 MINUTES

EQUIPMENT

- 11-inch fluted quiche dish
- strainer
- pastry brush
- small knife
- ladle
- baking sheet
- wire rack
- bowls
- pastry scraper
- whisk
- rolling pin

INGREDIENTS

- purple plums
- unsalted butter
- active dry yeast
- dried breadcrumbs
- flour
- eggs
- egg yolks
- heavy cream
- sugar
- vegetable oil

Bavaria is famous for its cakes and tarts. In this recipe, a quick version of brioche forms the base for a plum tart. Juice from the fruit mingles with the custard filling to bring about a deliciously moist result. The amount of sugar you need for sprinkling depends on the sweetness of the plums. Greengage plums, or apricots, are also delicious in this tart.

*plus 2¼–3 hours total rising time

SHOPPING LIST

1¾ lb	purple plums
2 tbsp	dried breadcrumbs
2	egg yolks
½ cup	sugar, more if needed
¼ cup	heavy cream
	For the brioche dough
1½ tsp	active dry yeast, or ½ cake (9 g) compressed yeast
¼ cup	lukewarm water
	vegetable oil for bowl
2 cups	flour, more if needed
2 tbsp	sugar
1 tsp	salt
3	eggs
½ cup	unsalted butter, more for quiche dish

ORDER OF WORK

1. **MAKE THE BRIOCHE DOUGH AND PIT THE PLUMS**

2. **LINE THE DISH AND FILL THE DOUGH SHELL**

3. **MAKE THE CUSTARD AND FINISH THE TART**

1 MAKE THE BRIOCHE DOUGH AND PIT THE PLUMS

1 Sprinkle or crumble the yeast over the water in a small bowl. Let stand until dissolved, 5 minutes. Lightly oil a medium bowl. Sift the flour onto the work surface. Make a well in the center and add the sugar, salt, yeast mixture, and eggs.

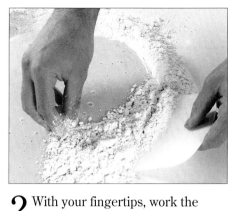

Circle of flour holds in wet ingredients

2 With your fingertips, work the ingredients in the well until they are thoroughly mixed. Draw in the flour with the pastry scraper.

3 Work the flour into the other ingredients with your fingertips to form a soft dough; work in more flour if it is very sticky.

Lifting dough is integral part of kneading process

4 Knead the dough on a floured work surface, lifting it up and throwing it down until it is very elastic and resembles chamois leather, about 10 minutes. Work in more flour as necessary, so that at the end of kneading the dough is slightly sticky but peels easily from the work surface.

Dough will become less sticky and more elastic during kneading

5 Pound the butter with the rolling pin to soften it. Add the butter to the dough; pinch and squeeze to mix it in, then knead the dough on the work surface until it is smooth again, 3–5 minutes. Alternatively, the dough can be kneaded and the butter added using an electric mixer with a dough hook.

Brioche dough should be satiny smooth

6 Shape the dough into a ball, and put it into the oiled bowl. Cover, and let rise in the refrigerator until doubled in bulk, 1½–2 hours. Meanwhile, pit the plums (see box, page 100). Cut each plum half in two.

ANNE SAYS
"If more convenient, the dough can be left to rise overnight in the refrigerator."

HOW TO HALVE AND PIT PLUMS

The riper the fruit, the more easily it separates from the pit.

1 With a small, sharp knife, cut a plum in half, following the indentation on one side as a guide.

2 Twist with both hands to loosen the plum halves; then pull them apart.

3 If the flesh clings, loosen it with the knife. Lift or scoop out the pit with the point of the knife; discard.

2 LINE THE DISH AND FILL THE DOUGH SHELL

1 Brush the quiche dish with melted butter. Knead the chilled brioche dough lightly to knock out the air. Flour the work surface; roll out the dough to a 13-inch round.

3 Lift the edge of the dough with one hand and press it into the bottom and up the side with the other hand.

Plum wedges will be arranged cut-side up to help excess juice evaporate

5 Sprinkle the breadcrumbs over the bottom of the dough shell. Arrange the plum wedges, cut-side up, in concentric circles on top. Let stand at room temperature until the edge of the dough is puffed, 30–45 minutes. Meanwhile, heat the oven to 425° F. Put the baking sheet in the oven to heat.

Dough is easy to drape with help of rolling pin

2 Wrap the dough around the rolling pin and loosely drape it over the quiche dish.

4 With the small knife, trim off the excess dough, using the rim of the dish as a guide.

ANNE SAYS
"Breadcrumbs absorb juice from the fruit so the brioche does not become soggy."

3 MAKE THE CUSTARD AND FINISH THE TART

1 Put the egg yolks and two-thirds of the sugar into a bowl. Pour in the heavy cream. Whisk the mixture together to combine.

2 Sprinkle the plum wedges with the remaining sugar, and bake the tart on the baking sheet in the heated oven, 5 minutes. Reduce the heat to 350°F.

3 Ladle the custard mixture over the fruit, return the tart to the oven, and continue baking until the dough is browned, the fruit is tender, and the custard is set, 45–50 minutes longer.

! TAKE CARE !
Do not overbake the tart, or the custard may curdle.

¶⊙ TO SERVE
Let the tart cool on the wire rack. Serve the tart warm or at room temperature, cut into wedges.

Sugared plums cook to a shiny glaze

VARIATION

BAVARIAN BLUEBERRY TART

Blueberries resemble European bilberries, a popular alternative to the plums in Bavarian Plum Tart. The tart is served sprinkled with confectioners' sugar.

1 Omit the plums. Prepare the brioche dough as directed. Pick over 2 pints blueberries, and wash them only if they are dirty. Leave the fruit whole.
2 Assemble the tart as directed. Make custard as directed, using 1/3 cup sugar, 4 egg yolks, and 1/2 cup heavy cream.
3 Sprinkle the blueberries with 2 tbsp sugar. Bake the tart, 5 minutes, as directed. Ladle the custard over the blueberries and bake the tart, 45–50 minutes longer.
4 Just before serving, use a strainer to sprinkle the tart with 1–2 tbsp confectioners' sugar. Serve the tart warm or at room temperature, cut into wedges.

— **GETTING AHEAD** —
The brioche dough can be prepared up to 1 day ahead and kept, covered, in the refrigerator. The tart is best eaten on the day of baking.

APPLE JALOUSIE

 SERVES 6–8   WORK TIME 1¼–1½ HOURS*   BAKING TIME 30–40 MINUTES

EQUIPMENT

rolling pin

chef's knife

pastry brush

large frying pan†

melon baller

vegetable peeler

wire rack

small knife

pastry scraper

baking sheet

strainer

chopping board

small strainer

whisk

wooden spoon

† large sauté pan can also be used

ANNE SAYS
"*Puff pastry dough must be kept cold when rolled, so a marble slab is ideal. Or, place a roasting pan filled with ice water on the work surface for 15 minutes. Dry the surface before rolling the dough.*"

In French, a jalousie *is a louvered shutter – perfect for the observance of wives by jealous husbands. In this golden pastry, the top layer of dough is slashed crosswise to look like a shutter, revealing glimpses of the apple compote inside. The filling is spiced with fresh ginger root, and the flavor is best when tart apples are used.*

GETTING AHEAD
The puff pastry dough can be given 4 turns, tightly wrapped, and refrigerated up to 2 days, or frozen up to 3 months. Complete the final 2 turns and bake the day of serving.

*plus 1¼ hours chilling time

SHOPPING LIST

2 lb	tart apples
1-inch	piece of fresh ginger root
1 tbsp	unsalted butter
½ cup	sugar
1	egg white
	For the puff pastry dough
2 cups	flour
1 cup	unsalted butter
1 tsp	salt
1 tsp	lemon juice
½ cup + 2 tbsp	water, more if needed

INGREDIENTS

apples

fresh ginger root

unsalted butter

flour

sugar

egg white

lemon juice

ANNE SAYS
"*If you wish, you can save 40–50 minutes work time by substituting 1 lb ready-prepared puff pastry dough for the homemade puff pastry dough used in the recipe.*"

ORDER OF WORK

1 MAKE THE PUFF PASTRY DOUGH; PREPARE THE FILLING

2 ASSEMBLE AND BAKE THE JALOUSIE

1 MAKE THE PUFF PASTRY DOUGH; PREPARE THE FILLING

1 Make and chill the puff pastry dough (see pages 104–105). Peel the apples with the vegetable peeler. Cut out the flower and stem ends from each apple.

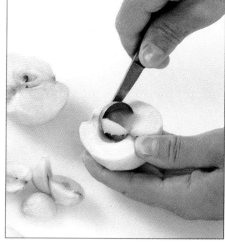

Minimum of apple flesh is removed with vegetable peeler

2 Halve the apples with the chef's knife, then scoop out the core from each half with the melon baller.

3 Set 1 apple half, cut-side down, on the chopping board. Cut it horizontally into ¼-inch slices.

4 Cut the slices lengthwise into ¼-inch strips. Gather the strips together in a pile and cut crosswise into dice. Repeat for the remaining apple halves.

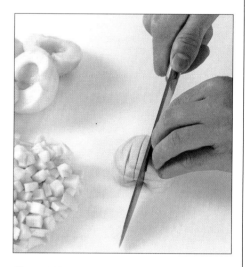

5 With the small knife, peel the skin from the fresh ginger root. With the chef's knife, slice the ginger, cutting across the fibrous grain. Crush each slice with the flat of the knife, then finely chop the slices.

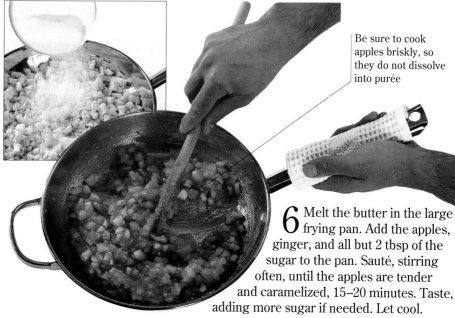

Be sure to cook apples briskly, so they do not dissolve into purée

6 Melt the butter in the large frying pan. Add the apples, ginger, and all but 2 tbsp of the sugar to the pan. Sauté, stirring often, until the apples are tender and caramelized, 15–20 minutes. Taste, adding more sugar if needed. Let cool.

HOW TO MAKE PUFF PASTRY DOUGH

Puff pastry dough is the lightest, and yet the richest, of all the pastry doughs. It is composed of literally hundreds of layers of dough interleaved with unsalted butter.

1 Sift the flour onto the work surface and make a well in the center. Cut 2 tbsp of the butter into pieces, and add to the well with the salt, lemon juice, and water.

2 Quickly blend the butter, salt, lemon juice, and water together in the well with your fingertips.

3 Gradually draw in the flour, working with your fingertips, to form coarse crumbs. If the crumbs seem dry, add a little more water to form a dough.

4 With a pastry scraper, cut and turn the dough several times until it forms a rough, slightly moist ball.

ANNE SAYS
"At this stage, try to handle the dough as little as possible."

Work with pastry scraper rather than hands, so dough remains cool

5 Score the dough with the pastry scraper to prevent shrinkage; then wrap and chill, 15 minutes.

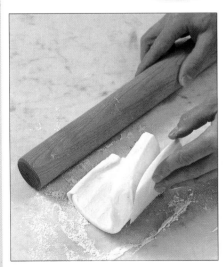

6 Lightly flour the remaining butter. Pound the butter with a rolling pin, folding and pounding it until it is softened and pliable.

ANNE SAYS
"The butter should be pounded until it is the same consistency as the dough, making it easy to roll them together."

7 With the pastry scraper, shape the piece of butter into a 5-inch square.

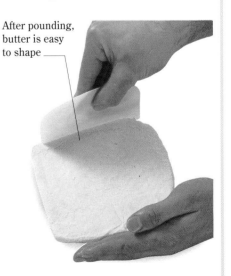

After pounding, butter is easy to shape

8 Roll out the chilled dough on a lightly floured work surface to a 10-inch square that is slightly thicker in the center than at the sides.

Wrap dough closely around butter

9 Set the square of butter diagonally in the center, and pull the corners of the dough around the butter to wrap it like an envelope. Pinch the edges together with your fingers to seal them.

10 Lightly flour the work surface again and turn the dough and butter package over onto it, seam-side down. Tap the package several times with the rolling pin, so that it becomes flattened.

Roll dough with firm, even pressure

11 Roll out the flattened dough to a rectangle about 6 inches wide and 18 inches long, keeping the corners square and the thickness even.

ANNE SAYS
"Work briskly and roll the dough away from you, keeping it moving on the floured surface."

12 Neatly fold the dough into three, bringing the top third down, and the bottom third up, like a business letter, so that it forms a square of dough.

13 Turn the dough square 90° to bring the seam-side to your right. Gently press the layered ends with the rolling pin to seal them. This completes the first turn. Repeat steps, 11, 12, and 13 to complete a second turn.

ANNE SAYS
"Each rolling out, folding, and pressing of the pastry dough is called a turn."

14 Mark the number of turns in one corner of the dough with your fingertips. Wrap the dough and chill, 15 minutes. Repeat 2 turns twice more to make a total of 6 turns, chilling the dough 15 minutes after each set of 2 turns.

2 ASSEMBLE AND BAKE THE JALOUSIE

1 Sprinkle the baking sheet with cold water. Lightly flour the work surface, then roll out the dough, and trim it into an 11- x 13-inch rectangle with the chef's knife.

Use sharp knife, so dough is cut cleanly

2 Cut the dough lengthwise in half. Fold one half lengthwise. Starting ³/₈-inch from the long edges, cut across the fold at ¹/₄-inch intervals.

3 Transfer the uncut rectangle of dough to the prepared baking sheet and press it down lightly. Spoon the apple filling evenly down the center, leaving a ³/₄-inch border.

4 Using the pastry brush, moisten the border of the dough with cold water.

Brush border of dough with water so lid can be sealed firmly to base

5 Line up 1 long edge of the slashed dough rectangle with 1 long edge of the rectangle on the baking sheet. Unfold the slashed dough over the filling.

When adding top layer of dough, match each edge carefully to base

6 Press the dough edges together with your fingertips. With a sharp knife, trim the edges to neaten them.

7 Holding the dough in place with one fingertip, scallop the edges at close intervals with the back of the small knife. Chill the jalousie, 15 minutes. Heat the oven to 425°F. Bake in the heated oven until puffed and brown, 20–25 minutes. Meanwhile, whisk the egg white just until it is frothy.

Back of small knife scores without cutting pastry edge

8 Brush the hot jalousie with the egg white, and sprinkle the remaining sugar evenly over the top through the small strainer. Return the jalousie to the oven, and continue baking until the sugar glaze is crisp and the pastry is deep golden, 10–15 minutes longer. Transfer the jalousie to the wire rack, and let cool.

¶○¶ TO SERVE

Cut the jalousie crosswise into 6–8 slices, and transfer to individual plates. Serve warm or at room temperature.

Crispy glaze comes from egg white and sugar

Caramelized apples are a delicious filling for puff pastry

VARIATION

BANANA SHUTTLES

These tartlets are called shuttles because they resemble the tools used by weavers at the loom.

1 Omit the apples and fresh ginger root. Make and chill the puff pastry dough as directed.

2 Combine ¼ cup sugar with ¼ tsp ground cinnamon and ¼ tsp ground cloves. Transfer the mixture to a sheet of parchment paper. Pour 3 tbsp dark rum into a shallow dish. Peel 3 medium bananas, and cut each one crosswise in half. Dip each banana half in the rum, then coat with the sugar mixture.

3 Sprinkle a baking sheet with water. Roll out the puff pastry dough, and trim it to a 12- x 15-inch rectangle. Cut the dough into twelve 3- x 5-inch rectangles. Fold 6 of the rectangles in half lengthwise, and make three ½-inch cuts across the fold of each one. Set the remaining rectangles on the prepared baking sheet, pressing them down lightly.

4 Cut each banana half into thin crosswise slices; then set the slices in the center of each puff pastry rectangle, leaving a ⅜-inch border around the edge. Brush the dough borders with cold water.

5 Line up and unfold the slashed rectangles over the filled bases. Press the dough edges with your fingertips to seal. Trim one end of each rectangle to a blunt point. Scallop the edges of the shuttles with the back of a small knife.

6 Chill the shuttles, 15 minutes, and bake them in the heated oven as directed, allowing 15–20 minutes cooking time before adding the glaze, then bake 10–15 minutes longer.

HAZELNUT, CHOCOLATE, AND ORANGE TART

🍽 SERVES 6–8   🥄 WORK TIME 45–50 MINUTES*   🍲 BAKING TIME 35–40 MINUTES

EQUIPMENT

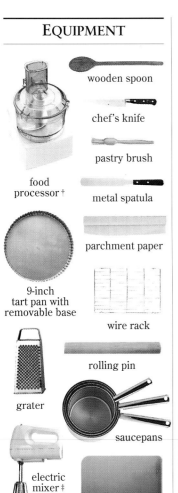

- wooden spoon
- chef's knife
- pastry brush
- food processor †
- metal spatula
- parchment paper
- 9-inch tart pan with removable base
- wire rack
- rolling pin
- grater
- saucepans
- electric mixer ‡
- baking sheet
- dish towel
- pastry scraper
- bowls
- strainer
- small knife
- vegetable peeler
- metal skewer

† rotary grater can also be used
‡ wooden spoon can also be used

Pasta frolla, the Italian sweet pie pastry, acts as a container for a rich filling flavored with ground hazelnuts, semisweet chocolate, and candied orange zest, topped with a chocolate glaze.
*plus 45 minutes chilling time

SHOPPING LIST

2	oranges
³/₄ cup	sugar
¹/₄ cup	water
1 cup	hazelnuts
2 oz	semisweet chocolate
²/₃ cup	unsalted butter
2 tsp	flour
2	egg yolks
1	egg
For the pasta frolla dough	
1	orange
1¹/₄ cups	flour, more if needed
¹/₃ cup	unsalted butter, more for tart pan
¹/₄ cup	sugar
¹/₄ tsp	salt
1	egg
For the chocolate glaze	
4 oz	semisweet chocolate
¹/₃ cup	unsalted butter
2 tsp	Grand Marnier

INGREDIENTS

- oranges
- Grand Marnier †
- sugar
- hazelnuts
- unsalted butter
- flour
- semisweet chocolate
- eggs
- egg yolks

† another orange-flavored liqueur can also be used

ORDER OF WORK

1 MAKE THE PASTA FROLLA DOUGH

2 LINE THE TART PAN

3 MAKE THE FILLING; BAKE THE TART

4 MAKE THE CHOCOLATE GLAZE; FINISH THE TART

MAKE THE PASTA FROLLA DOUGH

1 Grate the zest from the orange. Sift the flour onto the work surface, and make a well in the center.

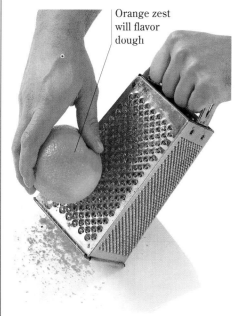

Orange zest will flavor dough

2 Pound the butter with the rolling pin to soften it, so that it blends in easily with the other ingredients.

3 Put the softened butter, the sugar, salt, orange zest, and egg into the well.

Softened butter will blend easily with sugar

Egg will bind dough together

4 With your fingertips, work the ingredients in the well until thoroughly mixed.

Fingertips gradually mix flour into wet ingredients

5 Draw in the flour with the pastry scraper, then work the flour into the other ingredients with your fingertips until coarse crumbs form. Press the dough into a ball. If it is sticky, work in a little more flour.

6 Lightly flour the work surface. Blend the dough by pushing it away from you with the heel of your hand, then gathering it up, until it is very smooth and peels away from the work surface in one piece, 1–2 minutes.

7 Shape the dough into a ball, wrap it tightly, and chill until firm, about 30 minutes.

Blended dough peels away in one piece

2 LINE THE TART PAN

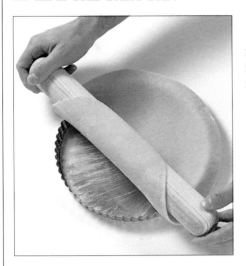

1 Brush the pan with melted butter. Lightly flour the work surface, and roll out the dough into an 11-inch round. Wrap the dough around the rolling pin, and drape it over the pan.

2 Gently lift the edge of the dough with one hand, and press it well into the bottom of the pan with the other hand, pressing to seal any cracks. Overlap the dough slightly inside the rim of the pan so extra dough is left at the edge of the shell.

Make fork holes close together

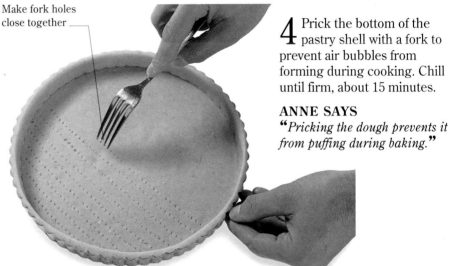

4 Prick the bottom of the pastry shell with a fork to prevent air bubbles from forming during cooking. Chill until firm, about 15 minutes.

ANNE SAYS
"Pricking the dough prevents it from puffing during baking."

3 Roll the rolling pin over the top of the pan, pressing down to cut off excess dough. With your thumbs, press the dough evenly up the side of the pan, from the bottom, to increase the height of the rim.

3 MAKE THE FILLING; BAKE THE TART

Pith is left behind when oranges are pared carefully

Cut orange zest into finest possible julienne strips

1 Candy the orange zest: with the vegetable peeler, pare the zest from the oranges; cut it into very fine julienne strips with the chef's knife.

2 Bring a small saucepan of water to a boil, add the strips of orange zest, and simmer, 2 minutes. Drain the strips in the strainer; set them aside.

HOW TO TOAST AND SKIN NUTS

Toasting nuts intensifies their flavor and adds crunch to their texture. It also makes it easier to remove thin skin from nuts such as hazelnuts. You can tell that they are toasted when the skins start to pop and the nuts smell fragrant.

1 Heat the oven to 350°F. Spread out the nuts on a baking sheet, and toast in the heated oven until they are just lightly browned, 6–15 minutes, depending whether they are whole or chopped, and on the type of nut. Stir occasionally, so the nuts color evenly.

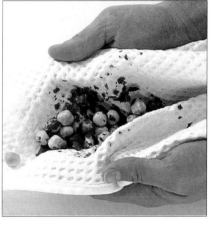

2 To remove skins from hazelnuts, rub in a dish towel while still hot. Discard the skins. Let cool.

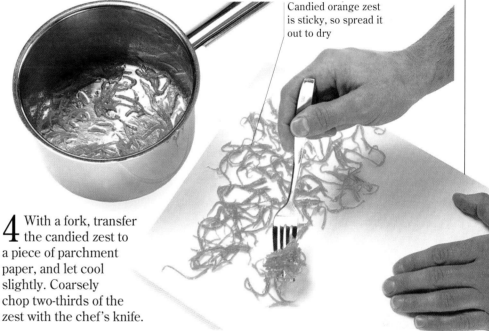

Candied orange zest is sticky, so spread it out to dry

3 Put one-third of the sugar into a pan, add the measured water, and heat gently until dissolved, shaking the pan once or twice. Add the zest strips, and simmer until all the water has evaporated, and the zest strips are transparent and tender, 8–10 minutes.

4 With a fork, transfer the candied zest to a piece of parchment paper, and let cool slightly. Coarsely chop two-thirds of the zest with the chef's knife.

5 Toast and skin the hazelnuts (see box, above). Let cool. Leave the oven temperature at 350°F, and put in the baking sheet to heat. Cut the chocolate into chunks, then finely chop with the chef's knife. Or, chop it in the food processor, using the pulse button.

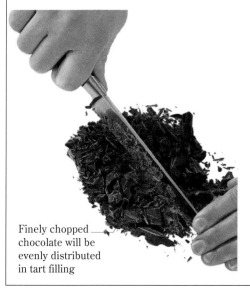

Finely chopped chocolate will be evenly distributed in tart filling

6 Put the remaining sugar in the food processor, add the hazelnuts, and finely grind. Or, grind just the nuts in a rotary grater, and mix with the sugar.

ANNE SAYS
"The sugar helps prevent the hazelnuts from becoming oily."

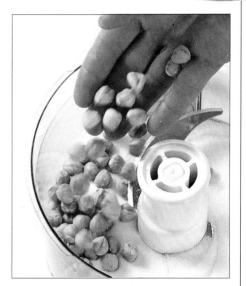

7 Beat the butter until creamy. Add the flour and the hazelnut mixture, and continue beating, until light and fluffy, 2–3 minutes. Add the yolks and egg, one at a time, beating after each addition. Mix in the chocolate and chopped candied orange zest.

Mix in each egg yolk thoroughly before adding whole egg

8 Spread the filling over the bottom of the pastry shell, and smooth the top. Bake the tart on the baking sheet in the heated oven until the metal skewer inserted in the center comes out clean, 35–40 minutes. Let the tart cool on the wire rack.

4 MAKE THE CHOCOLATE GLAZE; FINISH THE TART

Butter gives glaze glossy finish when spread on tart

1 While the tart is cooling, make the chocolate glaze. Cut the chocolate into chunks. Heat the chocolate in a bowl set over a saucepan of hot water, stirring occasionally, just until melted.

2 Cut the butter into small pieces, and gently stir it into the warm melted chocolate in 2–3 batches.

3 Add the Grand Marnier, and stir it into the chocolate mixture, adding more to taste. Let the glaze cool to tepid. Set the tart pan on a bowl to loosen and remove the side.

Leave border around glaze for decoration of candied zest

4 Pour the glaze onto the tart, and spread it smoothly over the center. With the edge of the metal spatula, carefully mark radiating lines in the glaze, holding the spatula in one hand and turning the tart with the other.

TO SERVE

Slide the tart from the pan base onto a plate. Decorate with the remaining candied orange zest. Cut the tart into wedges and serve at room temperature.

VARIATION
CHOCOLATE AND WALNUT TRUFFLE TART

In this version of Hazelnut, Chocolate, and Orange Tart, toasted walnuts take the place of hazelnuts in the filling – and some of them are reserved and coated in melted chocolate to decorate the tart. A topping of cocoa powder is sifted over the glazed tart to echo the coating for chocolate truffles.

1 Omit the hazelnuts, orange zest, sugar for candying, and candied orange zest. Make the pasta frolla dough, without the zest, and chill as directed. Line the tart pan, and chill the pastry shell as directed.

2 Toast 1¼ cups walnut halves as for the hazelnuts, but do not skin them. Reserve 8 halves for decoration. Grind the remaining nuts with ½ cup sugar as directed. Make the filling as directed, adding 1 tsp vanilla extract in place of the candied orange zest.

3 Bake the tart as directed, and let cool. Melt 6 oz semisweet chocolate as directed for the glaze. Dip the reserved walnut halves into the melted chocolate to coat completely; set aside.

4 Finish the glaze as directed, using the remaining melted chocolate. Glaze the top of the tart completely, without marking it in a pattern. Let cool.

5 Just before serving, sift 2–3 tbsp cocoa powder in a generous layer over the tart. Arrange the chocolate-coated walnut halves on top of the tart. Cut it into wedges, and serve at room temperature.

Orange and chocolate are a classic flavor combination

Chocolate glaze gives tempting finish

GETTING AHEAD

The dough can be made up to 2 days ahead and kept, tightly wrapped, in the refrigerator. The tart can be baked and stored up to 2 days in an airtight container, and the flavors will mellow. Add the glaze not more than 4 hours before serving.

PISTACHIO AND RICOTTA PHYLLO PIE

🍽 SERVES 6–8　🥄 WORK TIME 35–40 MINUTES　🍲 BAKING TIME 45–50 MINUTES

EQUIPMENT

pastry brush

kitchen scissors

small knife

food processor †

bowls

electric mixer ‡

aluminum foil

grater

8-inch square cake pan

small brush

rubber spatula

baking sheet

wire rack

saucepans

dish towels

† blender can also be used
‡ hand whisk can also be used

INGREDIENTS

ricotta cheese

shelled pistachio nuts

phyllo dough

ground cinnamon

sour cream

vanilla extract

light brown sugar

flour

unsalted butter

raisins

honey

granulated sugar

egg

lemons

Phyllo pastry is uniquely adaptable to many different shapes. Here, a giant box of layered phyllo dough is filled with alternating layers of ricotta cheese and ground pistachios, and finished with phyllo rosettes.

GETTING AHEAD
The baked pie can be kept in the refrigerator up to 2 days; allow it to come to room temperature before serving.

SHOPPING LIST

¹/₂ lb	package phyllo dough
¹/₂ cup	unsalted butter, more for cake pan
	For the pistachio and ricotta fillings
²/₃ cup	shelled pistachio nuts
3 tbsp	granulated sugar
3 tbsp	light brown sugar
2	lemons
1	egg
6 oz	ricotta cheese
¹/₃ cup	sour cream
1 tsp	vanilla extract
2 tbsp	honey
2 tsp	flour
	salt
¹/₃ cup	raisins
	For the topping
1 tsp	ground cinnamon
1 tbsp	granulated sugar

ANNE SAYS
"About 10 sheets of phyllo dough are needed for this recipe, but I always have a few extra in case some tear. Any remaining sheets can be wrapped tightly and frozen."

ORDER OF WORK

1 MAKE THE PISTACHIO AND RICOTTA FILLINGS

2 ASSEMBLE AND BAKE THE PIE

1 MAKE THE PISTACHIO AND RICOTTA FILLINGS

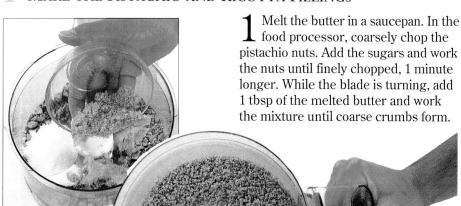

1 Melt the butter in a saucepan. In the food processor, coarsely chop the pistachio nuts. Add the sugars and work the nuts until finely chopped, 1 minute longer. While the blade is turning, add 1 tbsp of the melted butter and work the mixture until coarse crumbs form.

Grinding pistachios with sugar helps keep them from turning to paste

2 Finely grate the zest from each of the lemons, using the small brush to remove any zest remaining on the grater. Set aside. In a medium bowl, stir the egg. Add the ricotta cheese.

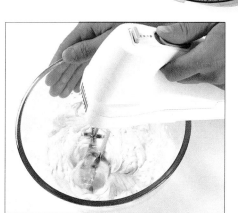

Filling combines classic Mediterranean ingredients

Honey is easier to measure if it is warmed first

4 Add the sour cream, lemon zest, vanilla extract, honey, flour, and a pinch of salt to the egg and ricotta mixture. Continue beating until the mixture is light and fluffy, 2–3 minutes. Stir in the raisins.

3 Beat the egg and ricotta cheese with the electric mixer, or with a hand whisk, until smooth.

2 ASSEMBLE AND BAKE THE PIE

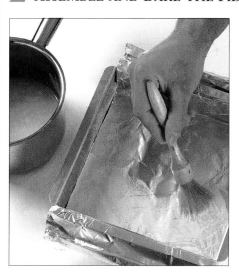

1 Heat the oven to 350°F. Put the baking sheet in the oven to heat. Brush the cake pan with melted butter; line with a strip of double thickness aluminum foil, draping the excess over the edges. Roll up the excess to form handles. Brush with melted butter.

2 Lay a dish towel on the work surface, and sprinkle it lightly with water. Unroll the phyllo dough sheets onto it. Trim the sheets to 8-x 16-inch rectangles. Cover the sheets and trimmings with a second dampened dish towel.

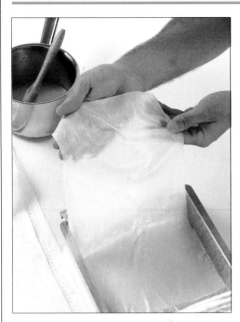

3 Put 1 of the sheets of dough on top of a third dampened dish towel, and brush with butter. Lay it in the bottom of the pan so that part of the sheet drapes over one edge of the pan.

Melted butter is essential in composition of pie

4 Butter a second sheet. Lay it in the bottom of the pan so that part drapes over the edge at right angles to the first sheet. Butter third and fourth sheets, laying and pressing them into the pan so the excess drapes over the remaining 2 sides. Cut the remaining sheets in half to make 8-inch squares; cover with the dampened dish towel.

Handle dough carefully so it does not tear

5 With the rubber spatula, spread one-half of the ricotta cheese filling evenly over the dough in the pan.

6 Butter 3 of the squares of phyllo dough and lay each one, butter-side up, over the filling in the pan.

7 Evenly distribute half of the nut mixture on top of the buttered dough.

Overhanging dough will be folded over filling, to seal it in

Make sure nut mixture is evenly spread over dough

8 Butter and layer 3 more squares of dough on top of the nut mixture. Layer the remaining cheese and nut fillings with the buttered phyllo dough, finishing the layering with 3 squares of buttered dough.

9 Fold the 4 overhanging pieces of dough neatly over the pie, and brush the top with butter. Cut the reserved trimmings into 2-inch-wide strips.

10 Curl the strips to form loose rosettes, and arrange on top of the pie. Combine the cinnamon and sugar in a small bowl.

11 Brush pie and rosettes with the remaining melted butter, and sprinkle the cinnamon and sugar over the top. Bake on the heated baking sheet until golden brown and flaky, and a metal skewer inserted into the center for 30 seconds is hot to the touch, 45–50 minutes. Let cool slightly in the pan. Transfer to the wire rack; let cool to room temperature. Discard the foil.

🍴 **TO SERVE**

Transfer the pie to a serving plate. Cut it into squares for serving, and set on individual plates.

Phyllo pastry contains crunchy nuts and smooth ricotta with juicy raisins

Crisp rosettes are an appealing finish

V A R I A T I O N

POPPY SEED PHYLLO PIE

Poppy seeds replace pistachios in this round phyllo pie.

1 Omit the pistachio filling, and cinnamon and sugar topping. Make the ricotta cheese filling as directed.
2 Put 2 oz poppy seeds in a bowl, pour over boiling water to cover, then let stand, 2 minutes. Drain. Reserve 1 tsp poppy seeds for sprinkling. Grind the remainder in a spice or coffee grinder.
3 In a saucepan, combine the ground poppy seeds with 1/4 cup milk. Bring just to a boil and simmer, 2 minutes. Off the heat, stir in 1/4 cup honey and 1/3 cup raisins. Transfer to a bowl and let cool. Beat 1 egg to mix, and stir it into the cool filling.
4 Melt the butter. Brush a 9-inch tart pan with a removable base with the melted butter. Lay a dish towel on the work surface and sprinkle it lightly with water. Unroll the phyllo dough sheets on the dish towel. Trim 4 sheets into 10- x 12-inch rectangles. Cover, butter, and layer at right angles to one another as directed.
5 Cut the remaining sheets in half, then into 9-inch rounds.
6 Fill and layer the pie as directed. Fold the overhanging pieces of dough over the filling, pleating them into a neat pattern around the edge.
7 Brush with the remaining butter, and sprinkle the reserved poppy seeds over the top. Bake as directed.
8 Let cool slightly, then set the pan on a bowl to loosen and remove the side. Slide the pie from the base onto a wire rack. Let cool to room temperature before setting on a serving plate.

Fresh Fruit Tartlets

🍽 SERVES 9　🥣 WORK TIME 1¾ HOURS*　🍲 BAKING TIME 35–40 MINUTES

EQUIPMENT

bowls

chef's knife

pastry brush

whisk

wire rack　small knife

metal spatula

pastry scraper

rolling pin

strainers

baking sheets

saucepans,
1 heavy-based
with lid

chopping board

Make the most of fresh colorful fruit in season in these crisp tartlets. If you wish, you can save 40–50 minutes work time by substituting 1 lb ready-prepared puff pastry dough for the homemade puff pastry dough used in the recipe.
plus 1¾ hours chilling time

SHOPPING LIST

1	small papaya, weighing about ½ lb
1	medium kiwi fruit
2	purple plums, total weight about 4 oz
2	yellow plums, total weight about 4 oz
	For the puff pastry dough
2 cups	flour
1 cup	unsalted butter
1 tsp	salt
1 tsp	lemon juice
½ cup + 2 tbsp	water, more if needed
1	egg plus ½ tsp salt for glaze
	For the pastry cream
1	vanilla bean
2 cups	milk
6	egg yolks
6 tbsp	sugar
¼ cup	flour
1 tbsp	unsalted butter
	For the apricot glaze
½ cup	apricot jam
1 tbsp	kirsch

INGREDIENTS

kiwi fruit　plums　papaya

flour

lemon juice

sugar

kirsch†

egg　egg yolks

apricot jam

milk

unsalted butter　vanilla bean‡

† water can also be used
‡ 1 tsp vanilla extract can also be used

ORDER OF WORK

1 MAKE THE DOUGH; SHAPE AND BAKE THE TARTLET SHELLS

2 MAKE THE PASTRY CREAM

3 PREPARE THE FRUIT, MAKE THE GLAZE, AND ASSEMBLE THE TARTLETS

1 MAKE THE DOUGH; SHAPE AND BAKE THE TARTLET SHELLS

1 Make and chill the dough (see pages 104–105). Make the egg glaze: lightly beat the egg with the salt. Sprinkle a baking sheet with water.

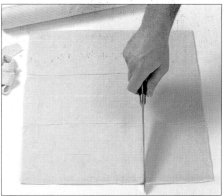

2 Lightly flour the work surface, then roll out the puff pastry dough, and trim it to a 15-inch square. With the chef's knife, cut the square into nine 5-inch squares.

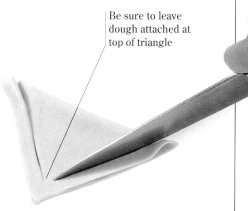

Be sure to leave dough attached at top of triangle

3 Fold 1 square in half to form a triangle. Cut a ½-inch border on the 2 unfolded edges of the triangle, leaving the dough attached at the top of the triangle.

4 Transfer the dough triangle to the prepared baking sheet, unfold, and press down lightly. Brush cold water around the edge of the inner square. Pick up a point of the border, lift, and flip it over to the opposite point of the inner square. Repeat with the remaining border so that a twist is formed at 2 corners of the square.

Point of border meets opposite point of inner square

5 With your fingertips, press the border firmly onto the dough beneath. Cut and place the borders for the remaining squares, using more baking sheets as necessary. Mark a "V" pattern on the border of each square with the back of the small knife, and scallop the edges. Prick the bottoms of the shells with a fork.

7 Bake the pastry shells, in batches as necessary, in the heated oven until starting to brown, 10–15 minutes. Reduce the oven temperature to 375°F, and if the dough has risen in the center, prick it again and press down with the back of a fork. Continue baking until the pastry is golden and very crisp, 5–10 minutes longer. Transfer the shells to the wire rack to cool.

6 Brush the borders of each shell with egg glaze, and chill until firm, 15 minutes. Heat the oven to 425°F.

Bake pastry very thoroughly, so it is deep golden

2 Make the Pastry Cream

Rub butter over surface of cream with fork

1 Split the vanilla bean, if using. In the heavy-based pan, bring the milk to a boil with the vanilla bean. Remove from the heat, cover, and let stand, 10–15 minutes. Whisk the egg yolks with the sugar until thick and light colored, 2–3 minutes. Add the flour, and stir it in with the whisk.

2 Gradually stir in the hot milk until the mixture is smooth. Pour it back into the saucepan. Bring to a boil over medium heat, whisking constantly until it thickens. Lower the heat, and cook the pastry cream, still whisking, until it softens slightly, about 2 minutes, to ensure the flour leaves no aftertaste.

3 Remove the pan from the heat, take out the vanilla bean, if using, or stir in the vanilla extract. Transfer to a bowl, then rub the butter over the surface of the cream to keep it from forming a skin. Chill, 30 minutes.

3 Prepare the Fruit, Make the Glaze, and Assemble the Tartlets

Papaya flesh will add vibrant color to tartlets

Spoon scoops out seeds easily

1 Cut the papaya lengthwise in half. Scoop out seeds. With the small knife, remove the skin; cut the papaya into thin wedges. Cut wedges crosswise in half.

2 Trim off the ends of the kiwi fruit. Set it upright, and peel off the skin in strips, working from top to bottom. Cut the fruit across into slices.

3 With the small knife, cut each plum in half, using the indentation on one side as a guide. Twist with both hands to loosen the plum halves; then pull them apart. Scoop out the pits with the point of the knife, and discard. Cut each plum half into thin wedges.

4 Make the glaze: heat the apricot jam with the kirsch in a pan, stirring, just until melted. Work through a strainer; melt again. Brush the bottom of each shell with glaze.

5 Spoon the pastry cream on top of the glaze in each pastry shell. Smooth the pastry cream with the back of the spoon.

6 Arrange some of the fruit wedges and slices on top of the pastry cream in a tartlet shell. Brush the fruit with glaze. Fill each of the remaining tartlet shells with fruit and brush with glaze.

Glaze fruit carefully so arrangement is not disturbed

🍽 TO SERVE
Transfer the tartlets to individual plates, and serve at room temperature.

Apricot glaze gives fruit a shine and keeps it from discoloring

GETTING AHEAD
The shells can be baked up to 1 day ahead and kept in an airtight container; pastry cream can be made up to 1 day ahead and kept, tightly covered, in the refrigerator. Assemble not more than 3 hours before serving.

VARIATION

MIXED BERRY TART
Here, the puff pastry dough is rolled out into a long strip, which is filled with Grand Marnier-flavored pastry cream, and topped with a trio of fresh berries arranged in long lines.

1 Make and chill the puff pastry dough as directed. Roll out half of the dough, and trim it to a 6- x 14-inch rectangle, or to the full length of your baking sheet. (Keep the remaining dough for another use.) Trim the edges. Cut a 3/4-inch strip from each long side of the rectangle. Transfer the rectangle to a dampened baking sheet. Brush cold water along a 1-inch border on each long edge of the rectangle, and set the strips on top to frame the edges. Brush the bottom of the rectangle and the frame with egg glaze. Chill, and bake the pastry shell as directed.

2 Make the pastry cream as directed. When the pastry cream is cool, stir in 1–2 tbsp Grand Marnier. Chill as directed.

3 Make the glaze as directed, using red currant jelly in place of apricot jam; do not work through a strainer. Pick over 3/4 pint strawberries, and 1/2 pint each of raspberries and blueberries, washing them only if dirty. Halve the strawberries if large.

4 Brush the bottom of the pastry shell with the red currant glaze, and spoon the pastry cream on top of the glaze. Arrange the mixed berries lengthwise in lines on top of the pastry cream, and brush with glaze.

5 Transfer the tart to a serving platter, and serve at room temperature, cut crosswise into slices.

PIES AND TARTS KNOW-HOW

No dessert is more appealing than a home-baked pie or tart. To make the most of your time in the kitchen, plan ahead. Be sure to check the section on "Getting Ahead" in each recipe because many preparations can be taken care of well in advance. Set aside time to find the finest and freshest ingredients. The quality and flavor of each ingredient – from the best chocolate to sun-ripened fruit – contribute to the success of your culinary efforts.

CHOOSING

The occasion is the first factor to consider when choosing an appropriate pie or tart. For a buffet, I like to make a selection of pies and tarts so that guests may choose their favorites. Recipes with contrasting colors and textures, such as Hazelnut, Chocolate, and Orange Tart, Pistachio and Ricotta Phyllo Pie, Lime and Cardamom Tart, and Mixed Berry Tart, are ideal, and they can either be cut into neat slices or squares. Every family loves Double-Crust Apple Pie, so serve it hot to end a casual supper at home, topped with a scoop of ice cream. Mud Pie, with swirls of fudge sauce, is sure to please any chocolate lover. For more formal dinners, Flaky Pear Tartlets, Apple Jalousie, or Caramelized Upside-Down Mango Tartlets would be appropriate.

The time of year is also a consideration – baking with the best a season offers is always a good idea. Late spring marks the start of the stone-fruit season, with cherries being some of the first to ripen. Cherry Tartlets is the perfect recipe for big, beautiful Bing cherries. From the summertime garden, there are baskets of berries and peaches. Show them off with plain and fancy favorites like Bavarian Blueberry Tart, Peach Pie with Walnut Pastry, and Fresh Fruit Tartlets. Naturally, autumn is the perfect season to bake Amelia Simmons' Molasses Pumpkin Pie. And when the cold winter months arrive, Fresh Mincemeat Tart served with Whiskey Hard Sauce, Fig and Mulled Wine Tart, and Triple-Decker Prune Tart are delicious – especially by the fire with family and friends.

DECORATING AND PRESENTING

Just a small decorative touch on a pie or tart can make all the difference; for example, a quick sprinkling of confectioners' sugar, or a golden brushing of egg glaze. In each recipe you will see how to neaten and decorate pastry edges, or how to dress up the top with shapes cut from pastry trimmings. Included are instructions on how to shape a pastry rose, how to create a lattice topping, how to make maple-leaf shapes, and how to make an impressive pastry braid.

Before baking a pie, I always think about how it will look on the table, and then try to choose an attractive dish. I put pie plates on carefully chosen platters – rustic, elegant, contemporary, depending on the occasion. When serving a pie or tart on a buffet table set with a number of other dishes, you can use a cake stand so the pie is raised. There are many attractive glass and ceramic stands available, both new and antique.

An important factor when serving pies and tarts is temperature. The flavor of creamy fillings and aromatic fruit pies can vary significantly, depending on whether they are served chilled or room temperature.

Pies and tarts can be served plain or with a number of accompaniments. You will find that I've made many suggestions in the recipes for appropriate sauces, creams, or ice creams. A sauce may be as simple as a fruit purée, such as the mango coulis served with Caramelized Upside-Down Mango Tartlets. The Whiskey Hard Sauce that I suggest serving with Fresh Mincemeat Tart takes only a little more time to prepare, and works very well with a warm tart like this. Crème fraîche pairs nicely with a rich recipe like Pear Pie with Walnut Pastry. Sweetened flavored whipped cream (Chantilly cream) is the perfect foil for the fruit- or nut-filled pies – Classic Pecan Pie is a good example. And of course there is ice cream. Pies and tarts that are served *à la mode* are an American tradition. Try Peach Pie with Walnut Pastry with a generous scoop of vanilla or your favorite nut-flavored ice cream, or Triple-Decker Dried Peach Tart with lemon sorbet.

DECORATIVE EDGES

It is surprisingly easy to give your pies and tarts a professional and eye-catching finish. By simply using your fingers, kitchen scissors, or a knife, you can shape or snip the pastry dough edge into the decoration of your choice. The edges illustrated here are just three examples of the possible decorative edges.

SCALLOPED EDGE

Double-crusted pies are ideal for making a scalloped edge; the double layer of pastry dough is easy to pinch into a neat decoration, and it catches juice that may seep from the pie filling.

1 With a small knife, trim the top crust even with the bottom crust. Press the edges together to seal them.

2 Place the forefinger of one hand on the edge of the dough, pointing outward. With the forefinger and thumb of your other hand, push the dough inward to form a scallop. Continue around the edge of the pie in this way until the scalloping is completed.

FLUTED EDGE

The edge of a single-crusted pie is built up so that it can be shaped into the decoration of your choice. Here, a quick pinch with your thumbs will transform plain pastry dough into an attractive fluted design.

1 Fold under the excess dough at the edge of the shell, then bring up above the pie plate rim to make an edge with a double thickness of dough.

2 Lightly press your thumbs together diagonally into the edge of the dough to make a ridge. Continue around the edge of the shell in this way until the fluting is completed.

FEATHERED EDGE

For a more elegant finish, snip the pastry dough with a pair of kitchen scissors. The feathered edge is delicate after baking, so handle the finished pie carefully to keep the pastry intact.

1 Pinch the dough edge between your thumb and forefinger to make it stand up. With scissors, make $1/2$-inch diagonal cuts at $1/2$-inch intervals around the edge of the shell.

2 With your fingertips, gently push one point toward the center of the shell, and the next point toward the edge of the shell. Continue around the edge of the shell in this way until the feathering is completed.

TECHNIQUES

In this volume, you can learn how to make 11 different pastries – light American pie pastry and its English counterpart, shortcrust pastry, are among them. French pâte brisée is thin yet robust, with a crumbly sweet version called pâte sucrée. You'll find orange-flavored Italian pasta frolla, several nut pastries, crisply layered puff pastry, buttery brioche yeast dough, and an unusual pastry containing cornmeal. You will become accomplished at lining pie plates and tart pans so the pastry dough does not shrink.

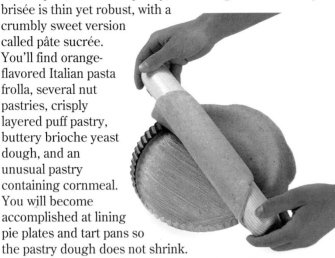

The pans I have chosen for these pies and tarts vary in shape and size. When lining a pan with pastry dough, it is important to use the proper technique. Stretching the dough can cause it to shrink during baking. When shaped correctly, the dough will not shrink or slide down the side of the pan. The method used for lining straight-sided French-style tart pans varies slightly from the technique we suggest for sloping-sided American pie plates. For both, quick and careful handling of the dough is mandatory if the finished pastry is to be light. For pies and tarts with a moist filling, the pastry shell is often partially baked before the filling is added to prevent the dough from becoming soggy. In some cases, the shell is completely baked before the filling is added. This step, which is called blind baking, is standard for both pies and tarts. Instructions are given for lining and weighing down the pastry shell so the dough keeps its shape during blind baking. One last caution, be sure to chill the pastry shell thoroughly before it goes into the oven.

Adding decorations to your pies and tarts will become second nature, as will a brushing of glaze or a sprinkling of sugar. I've included instructions for simple edges, such

as marking the dough by pressing with the tines of a fork or the edge of a spoon; you can also crimp and scallop the edge with your fingers, or make an impressive braid from strips of dough. To give pastry lids a lift, you'll see how to make leaves, roses, and berries from dough trimmings. Open tarts may be embellished with a woven pastry lattice, sealed at the edges so the strips do not shrink, or you may add some delicate white chocolate leaves, strawberry fans, or candied lemon slices.

Techniques you will come across when making fillings include preparing fruit, from everyday apples, oranges, and pears to tropical mangoes and fresh figs, toasting and chopping nuts, and melting chocolate and gelatin.

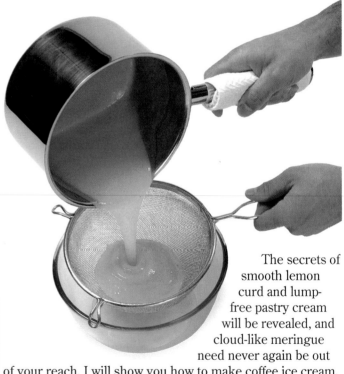

The secrets of smooth lemon curd and lump-free pastry cream will be revealed, and cloud-like meringue need never again be out of your reach. I will show you how to make coffee ice cream, and how to dress it up with swirls of fudge sauce with chopped nuts. You will see how simple it can be to make golden caramel sauce and smooth mango coulis – delicious with an assortment of desserts.

GETTING AHEAD

Pastry doughs benefit from being made ahead. All need to rest in the refrigerator at least 15 minutes before they are rolled out, and, if tightly wrapped, they can be refrigerated up to 2 days, or frozen up to 3 months. Puff pastry should be taken to 4 "turns" before storage, then turned twice more just before using. Let the dough come almost to room temperature before rolling it out.

You may find it easier to roll out and shape dough before storage, and in this case it can be baked straight from the refrigerator. If freezing shaped pastry shells, lids, or shapes, freeze them in the plate or pan or on the baking sheet until hard, then unmold and wrap them tightly. Defrost them, 1–2 hours, in the refrigerator before baking.

Freshly baked pastry is incomparable, but pie shells made of richer dough, such as puff pastry or pâte sucrée, can be kept, 1–2 days, in an airtight container without harm.

How long you can keep a finished pie depends very much on the filling. A moist filling of custard or fresh fruit can soften even crisply baked pastry within an hour or two. However, a tart with a firmer filling, such as Hazelnut, Chocolate, and Orange Tart, holds well up to 2 days. You'll find instructions for getting ahead with each recipe.

MICROWAVE COOKING

Baking pastry is not one of the strong points of a microwave oven. However, it can be used for cooking the crumb crusts of Mud Pie and Gingersnap Ice Cream Pie, and the almond crust of Chocolate Pye with a Crunchy Crust and its two accompanying variations.

A microwave oven can also help speed the melting of chocolate and gelatin. Medium power is recommended for melting chocolate, and timing depends on the output of your microwave oven, the type, and the amount of chocolate. For instance, 2 oz chopped semisweet chocolate takes about 2 minutes on Medium power. Coconut, and nuts, such as almonds, hazelnuts, and walnuts can be toasted on High. Use the microwave oven, too, to melt butter for brushing your pie plates and tart pans.

HOW-TO BOXES

In **Perfect Pies and Tarts** *you'll find pictures of all the techniques used in the recipes. However, some basic preparations appear in a number of recipes in special "how-to" boxes:*

INDEX

ACKNOWLEDGMENTS

Photographers David Murray
Jules Selmes
Photographer's Assistant Stephen Head

Chef Eric Treuille
Cookery Consultant Martha Holmberg
Home Economist Sarah Lowman

US Editor Jeanette Mall

Typesetting Linda Parker
Text film by Disc to Print (UK) Ltd

Production Consultant Lorraine Baird

*Anne Willan would like to thank her
chief editor Hilaire Walden and
associate editor Jacqueline Bobrow for
their vital help with writing the book
and researching and testing the
recipes, aided by Jane Reilly and
Joanna Rend and La Varenne's
chefs and trainees.*